The Shell Game

How Industrial Decay Ended America's Strategic Depth.

By Maria Perera Burrell

For Steven
on our wedding day, October 21, 2025.

For permission requests, contact the author at:
mariaperera.ax@gmail.com

The analysis and statistics presented in this book are based on publicly available sources believed to be reliable at the time of writing. They are provided for informational purposes only and may evolve as new data emerges. The author assumes no liability for any errors or omissions. All views expressed are the author's own and do not represent any institution or government.

Table of contents

Preface

Chapter 1: The Shell Shortage Revolution

Chapter 2: The Production Paradox

Chapter 3: The New Metrics of Military Power

Chapter 4: The Mobilization Impossibility

Chapter 5: Commercial Supply Chain Vulnerabilities

Chapter 6: The Drone Revolution and Asymmetric Manufacturing

Chapter 7: Strategic Implications and the Future of Military Power

Chapter 8: The Hidden Mathematics of Allied Burden

Chapter 9: The Bureaucratic Bottleneck: When Industrial Dysfunction Meets Strategic Necessity

Chapter 10: The Dependency Paradox: Adversary Components in American Arsenals

Chapter 11: Policy Prescriptions Overcoming the Mobilization Impossibility and Production Paradox

Conclusion: The Invariant Equation Of Strategic Sustainability

PREFACE

This book exists because Western defense establishments are operating under assumptions that no longer correspond to reality. For three decades following the Cold War, military planners in the United States and Europe have structured their forces, procurement strategies, and alliance commitments around a conceptual framework that treats industrial capacity as effectively infinite, a background condition rather than a binding constraint on military operations. The Ukraine conflict has rendered this assumption obsolete. The rate at which munitions are consumed now far exceeds Western replenishment capacity, exposing industrial speed, not intent, as the limiting variable of power.

The analysis that follows is not a technological assessment, nor is it primarily concerned with tactics, doctrine, or force structure in the traditional sense. Instead, it examines the mathematics of sustained military operations: the relationship between consumption rates and production capacity, the temporal dynamics of surge manufacturing, and the supply chain dependencies that determine whether sophisticated weapons systems can actually be employed at scale during prolonged conflicts. This is a field-manual view of power in a rate-limited world, where the fundamental question is not what forces can accomplish in the opening weeks of a conflict, but what they can sustain over months and years when stockpiles are exhausted and replenishment depends on industrial capacity that may be inadequate to the task. This is not a book about war, it is a book about what makes war sustainable.

The impetus for this examination came from observing the systematic disconnect between public discourse about military assistance to Ukraine and the underlying industrial realities that constrain what is actually deliverable. Political leaders announce ambitious targets for ammunition production. Defense officials emphasize cumulative aid totals. Yet these pronouncements consistently obscure the mathematical relationship between daily consumption rates and annual production capacity, a relationship that determines strategic sustainability far more than any single metric of total assistance provided.

What became apparent through research was that the constraints on Western ammunition production are not primarily financial, nor are they fundamentally technological. The United States and its European allies possess the economic resources and technical knowledge to produce artillery shells, precision munitions, and associated systems at substantially higher rates than current output. The binding constraints are instead structural: regulatory frameworks optimized for peacetime efficiency, workforce pipelines that cannot be rapidly expanded, supply chains dependent on geographically concentrated inputs, and organizational architectures that impede rather than facilitate rapid scaling.

These structural constraints have profound strategic implications because they operate on timescales that exceed the duration of most military operations. A regulatory approval process that requires eighteen months cannot be compressed to eighteen days simply because operational urgency demands faster action. A skilled workforce that requires two years of training cannot be conjured into existence when conflicts begin. Supply chains that depend on single-source suppliers in potentially hostile nations cannot be restructured overnight when geopolitical circumstances shift. The temporal asymmetries between the speed at which modern militaries consume munitions and the speed at which industrial systems can scale production create vulnerabilities that adversaries with different industrial models can exploit.

The analysis draws extensively on government oversight reports, procurement data, production statistics, and official assessments precisely because the most damning evidence about Western industrial capacity limitations comes not from external critics but from governments' own auditors and investigators. The Government

Accountability Office, the Congressional Research Service, and equivalent bodies in European nations have documented with remarkable clarity the organizational dysfunctions, supply chain vulnerabilities, and mobilization constraints that this book examines. These are not speculative concerns or theoretical vulnerabilities, they are empirical findings based on extensive reviews of actual procurement practices, facility inspections, and interviews with officials responsible for managing defense production.

The book is structured to move from specific empirical observations about ammunition shortages in Ukraine toward broader assessments of how industrial capacity shapes strategic possibility. Early chapters document the mathematics of production versus consumption and the structural reasons why Western manufacturing cannot rapidly scale. Middle chapters examine supply chain dependencies, technological disruptions, and organizational pathologies that compound these limitations. Later chapters explore strategic implications and policy responses. The progression is deliberate: establishing the factual foundation before drawing conclusions about what these constraints mean for deterrence, alliance commitments, and the future of military power. Each chapter can be read independently, but together they form a systems-level diagnosis of how rate, time, and scale govern strategic sustainability.

This is fundamentally a book about limits, the limits of what peacetime-optimized industrial systems can achieve when confronted with wartime demands, the limits of what democratic regulatory frameworks permit during emergencies, and the limits of what sophisticated militaries can accomplish when the industrial foundations supporting their operations prove inadequate. Acknowledging these limits is not defeatism but rather a prerequisite for developing strategies that align operational commitments with industrial realities. The alternative, continuing to plan as though industrial capacity can automatically expand to meet any requirement, risks discovering these constraints only when conflicts have already begun and options for mitigation have narrowed considerably.

The audience for this analysis includes defense professionals, policy makers, military officers, and informed citizens who recognize that understanding modern warfare requires examining not only battlefield capabilities but also the industrial systems that sustain them. The material is technical where precision demands it but aims throughout for clarity over jargon. The stakes are too high for the analysis to remain confined to specialist circles. Democratic publics that will ultimately determine whether their governments make the investments necessary to address industrial capacity constraints deserve accessible explanations of what those constraints are and why they matter.

Chapter 1
The Shell Shortage Revolution

The trajectory of the Ukraine conflict has exposed profound and uncomfortable truths about the relationship between industrial capacity and military effectiveness that Western defense establishments have long been reluctant to acknowledge. From the outset of the war, Ukrainian forces consumed artillery shells at rates that were previously unimaginable for European planners, with open-source reporting suggesting that during peak combat periods in 2022, Ukrainian artillery units fired between 6,000 and 8,000 shells per day. These consumption rates quickly revealed the limitations of European manufacturing infrastructure, which had been optimized for peacetime efficiency rather than wartime surge. Facilities that could comfortably meet training and ceremonial requirements were suddenly incapable of producing ammunition at the scale required for sustained high-intensity conflict.

The misalignment between consumption and production was not a result of technological backwardness. European defense contractors possess decades of experience producing precision munitions, including artillery shells, guided rockets, and electronic fuzes that meet exacting NATO standards. Rather, the structural shortfall lay in deliberate industrial choices. Following the Cold War, Western defense industrial policy prioritized cost efficiency, lean operations, and the elimination of "excess" capacity. Factories were calibrated to peacetime demand, and spare capacity was treated as unnecessary overhead rather than strategic insurance. This optimization logic, rational in a context of low-intensity interventions and limited conflicts, became a liability when Ukrainian forces required sustained and intensive artillery fire over months rather than weeks.

The economic rationale for these decisions was internally consistent: maintaining large-scale surge manufacturing capacity incurs significant fixed costs. For decades, European defense ministries justified investment in advanced aircraft, next-generation armored vehicles, and sophisticated command, control, communications, computers, intelligence, surveillance, and reconnaissance (C4ISR) systems, while accepting limited ammunition reserves as a manageable risk. The post-Cold War strategic environment reinforced these choices. Analysts assumed that any potential conflict with a peer adversary would be short, decisive, and technologically mediated, mirroring Western interventions in the 1990s Balkans campaigns, the Gulf War, or Afghanistan. These assumptions, however, proved catastrophically misaligned with the realities of attritional warfare in Ukraine.

As Ukrainian consumption of shells accelerated during 2022 and early 2023, the limitations of this peacetime-oriented industrial structure became starkly apparent. The European Union's ammunition plan, announced in March 2023, promised one million rounds for Ukraine within twelve months and a ramp-up to two million rounds per year by 2025. By late 2023, however, only 300,000 rounds had been delivered from existing stockpiles, with 180,000 more ordered from manufacturers. Progress accelerated substantially through 2024: by December 2024, the EU had delivered one million shells, fulfilling its initial pledge, though this came roughly nine months later than the original March 2024 target. By early 2025, most of the two million shell target had been achieved, demonstrating both the feasibility of scaling production and the extended timelines required to do so.

However, even these achievements illustrate the fundamental constraint. At the documented Ukrainian consumption rate of 6,000–8,000 shells per day during peak operations in 2022, even the target of two million rounds annually would cover only 34–46 percent of peak daily artillery usage. The mathematics are unforgiving:

sustaining peak operations would exhaust an entire year's production in approximately 250–333 days, leaving little buffer for operational flexibility or replenishment of domestic stockpiles. By 2025, Ukrainian consumption had declined significantly, not by choice but by necessity. By May 2025, Ukraine was receiving approximately 3,700 shells per day from the EU, and the fire ratio stood at 1:3, with Ukraine firing one round for every three Russian shells. These figures reveal that the EU's political promises, while representing genuine industrial mobilization, remain fundamentally constrained by the asymmetry between Western production capacity and adversary output.

The Ukraine conflict thus shifted the strategic problem from logistics management to industrial mathematics. Whereas previous conflicts were often limited by transportation bottlenecks or battlefield losses, the limiting factor in Ukraine became the rate of production itself. This distinction is critical. Stockpiles, no matter how large, are finite; replenishment requires time, materials, skilled labor, and regulatory approval. These constraints illustrate a fundamental tension between democratic governance, with its regulatory, safety, and environmental standards, and the operational imperatives of wartime production. European factories faced not only technical scaling issues but also bureaucratic and legal obstacles that slowed production expansions. Environmental permits, safety inspections, and workforce certifications, appropriate in peacetime, became severe bottlenecks when production needed to surge.

Human capital emerged as an equally intractable constraint. Modern munitions manufacturing is highly specialized, requiring precision machining, explosives handling, metallurgical expertise, and quality control proficiency. Unlike assembly-line consumer goods, these skills cannot be rapidly taught; they require months or years of apprenticeship and hands-on experience. The downsizing of defense manufacturing workforces over the past three decades, combined with demographic trends indicating declining participation in skilled trades, created acute shortages. U.S. Bureau of Labor Statistics projections indicate that by 2030, the United States alone could face 2.1 million unfilled manufacturing positions, a problem mirrored across Europe in specialized defense trades. Even with unlimited funding, the rate at which new skilled workers can be trained is limited, creating a human capital bottleneck that production automation alone cannot resolve.

The fragility of supply chains compounded these constraints. Critical inputs for artillery production,high-grade steel, propellant chemicals, electronic fuzes, and rare-earth components, are concentrated in a limited number of facilities and dependent on complex international supply networks. For instance, the specialized steel used in shell casings often comes from a small number of European foundries, and any disruption, whether political, environmental, or logistical, can have cascading effects on output. Similarly, modern proximity fuzes rely on microelectronics and semiconductor components tied to global supply chains, some of which are dependent on Chinese and other non-allied suppliers. This creates strategic vulnerability: production cannot be scaled independently of global industrial dependencies.

The consequences extend beyond Ukraine. NATO and U.S. military planning has long assumed that Western industrial bases can sustain multiple simultaneous high-intensity operations. Yet the Ukraine conflict empirically demonstrates that even a single sustained engagement can strain alliance production capacity to its breaking point. Each Javelin missile, HIMARS rocket, or guided artillery shell transferred to Ukraine reduces stockpiles available for potential contingencies in the Baltics, Eastern Mediterranean, or Indo-Pacific. Replacement timelines for complex systems such as Patriot batteries or advanced air-to-air missiles can extend up to two years, creating temporal asymmetries in operational sustainability.

The strategic asymmetry becomes more pronounced when examining adversary production models. Estimates suggest that Russia, even accounting for international sanctions and supply chain disruptions, produces in approximately three months what NATO alliance members collectively produce in a year. However, this calculation requires significant nuance: by 2024, Russia's domestic production capacity was estimated at approximately 2.3 million artillery shells annually. Russia's ability to sustain higher consumption rates, firing up to 7 million rounds in 2024, relied heavily on North Korean supplies, which comprised over 50 percent of monthly Russian consumption by mid-2024. Reports from Western intelligence and South Korean defense officials indicate that North Korea supplied between 3 million and 8 million shells to Russia between 2023 and 2025. This dependency reveals that Russia cannot sustain its usage rates through domestic production alone, though the combined production of Russia and North Korea still significantly outpaces NATO's collective output.

This strategic asymmetry reflects decades of industrial organization prioritizing surge capability over peacetime efficiency. While Western production has scaled significantly, the U.S., for instance, increased 155mm shell production from approximately 14,000 per month in early 2022 to over 40,000 per month by October 2024, with targets to reach 100,000 per month by late 2025 or 2026, these increases still fall short of the combined adversary output. The temporal dimension matters critically: Western production increases require multi-year investments in facilities, workforce training, and supply chain development, while adversaries maintain excess capacity that can be activated more rapidly.

The strategic implications of this mathematical asymmetry are profound. Western forces must consider operational tempo not merely in terms of tactical objectives but also in terms of sustainable production rates. Ukrainian commanders, aware of shell scarcity, have already adapted tactics to conserve limited resources, altering operational decisions based on anticipated replenishment timelines.

Similarly, NATO planners must consider that simultaneous crises, Ukraine, Taiwan, or other potential theaters, could force impossible choices between competing commitments, with alliance credibility and deterrence stability at stake.

Finally, the Ukraine conflict challenges the long-held belief that Western democracies can automatically translate economic power into military capacity. While Western economies are vast, their industrial bases remain heavily compartmentalized, regulated, and optimized for peacetime efficiency. China's Military-Civil Fusion approach, by contrast, integrates civilian manufacturing capacity into military production, creating flexibility that Western industrial models cannot match. This structural difference underscores a critical reality: long-term strategic competition is increasingly constrained not by technology alone, but by the mathematics of production, workforce development, and supply chain resilience.

The shell shortage revolution in Ukraine thus represents more than a logistical anomaly; it is a strategic inflection point. It exposes the fragility of Western defense industrial policy, highlights the human and material bottlenecks constraining sustained high-intensity operations, and forces a reevaluation of military doctrine, alliance assumptions, and the nature of deterrence in the twenty-first century. If democratic societies fail to reconcile industrial capacity with operational requirements, the consequences for future conflicts may be determined not on battlefields, but in the factories, supply chains, and workforce pipelines that underpin the art of modern war.

Chapter 2
The Production Paradox

The structural realities of defense manufacturing in advanced economies reveal a paradox that has remained largely unacknowledged until the Ukraine conflict forced these questions into sharp relief. For decades, defense industrial bases in Europe and North America have been optimized for efficiency, cost control, and technological sophistication rather than for the surge capacity required to sustain high-intensity, attritional warfare. This optimization reflects a series of rational decisions by governments, contractors, and procurement authorities, each of which made sense in isolation but collectively produced a system incapable of meeting the demands revealed by prolonged combat operations in Eastern Europe. The Ukraine conflict has therefore exposed the deep misalignment between the economic logic underpinning defense production and the strategic imperatives of modern warfare.

Since the end of the Cold War, Western defense manufacturing has increasingly focused on producing small quantities of technologically sophisticated platforms with long development cycles and exacting performance standards. Fighter aircraft, advanced armored vehicles, and precision-guided munitions became the focal points of investment, with production lines designed to operate continuously at a steady, predictable pace. The business model incentivized contractors to deliver high-value systems that commanded stable profit margins rather than simple munitions produced in mass quantities. This created a classic competency trap: industrial systems and workforces became highly proficient at meeting peacetime requirements while losing the capacity to respond to sudden surges in demand.

Artillery shells provide one of the clearest illustrations of this paradox. While the physics and metallurgy underlying shells have changed little over the past century, the requirements for modern manufacturing have become far more complex. High-quality steel with precise metallurgical properties, propellant chemicals produced under stringent safety standards, and increasingly sophisticated electronic components for proximity fuzes all create dependencies on extended supply chains. These supply chains are optimized for stable, predictable production and are often concentrated geographically in limited facilities, exposing them to vulnerability in the event of conflict. For example, semiconductors used in modern fuzes are produced in specialized foundries operated by a small number of companies, primarily Taiwan Semiconductor Manufacturing Company (TSMC) and Samsung, which control over 90 percent of advanced node production (below 10 nanometers) and maintain lead times for specialized military integrated circuits ranging from six to twelve months. The production of what would once have been considered a simple munition now depends on a global supply network optimized for commercial efficiency rather than military surge requirements.

The reliance on foreign supply chains extends beyond semiconductors. Rare earth elements, which are essential for precision munitions and electronic components, remain overwhelmingly sourced from China, which controls roughly 80 percent of global processed output. Specialized chemicals for rocket propellants, high-strength aluminum alloys for aircraft, and precision steel for shell casings are similarly concentrated in facilities optimized for cost-effective, steady-state production rather than rapid expansion. Environmental and safety regulations in Western countries further constrain the ability to scale production quickly. Processes that would allow increased throughput often require months or years of regulatory review, including environmental impact assessments, permitting for chemical handling, and compliance with labor safety standards. These constraints, while legitimate in peacetime, impose strategic limits in a crisis.

Labor represents an equally constraining factor. Munitions production requires highly skilled workers with experience in explosives handling, precision machining, and quality control procedures. The workforce capable of performing these tasks has shrunk significantly since the end of the Cold War, as declining production volumes discouraged new entrants and older workers retired. Many remaining workers entered the industry during the 1980s, creating an age distribution that concentrates expertise among individuals approaching retirement. Training new workers is a multi-year endeavor, requiring extensive apprenticeships, security clearances, and safety certification. Unlike commercial manufacturing, mistakes in munitions production can have catastrophic consequences, meaning that the workforce cannot be rapidly expanded without compromising safety. Security clearance backlogs, such as the approximately 300,000 pending cases in the U.S. Defense Counterintelligence and Security Agency as of 2024, further slow the process.

These human capital constraints interact with regulatory requirements and financial incentives in ways that compound the production paradox. Extended shifts or accelerated schedules are limited by safety laws, while environmental regulations prevent rapid expansion of facilities. Shareholders and corporate boards evaluating private defense contractors prioritize steady profits and risk minimization over the ability to surge production in a crisis. Maintaining idle capacity is financially inefficient, creating a collective action problem: no individual actor has sufficient incentive to maintain surge capability, and governments have largely moved away from owning production facilities since the privatization waves of the 1990s. Public arsenals and depots that once ensured industrial resilience were dismantled, leaving the system dependent on a private sector optimized for peacetime efficiency rather than wartime necessity.

The consequences of this production paradox are both immediate and strategic. NATO allies attempting to support Ukraine discovered that European shell production, even when fully mobilized, initially fell short of Ukrainian consumption rates during peak operations. The EU's target of two million artillery rounds annually, while representing genuine industrial mobilization and eventually achieved by early 2025, would supply only a fraction of the 6,000–8,000 rounds per day reportedly expended during peak operations in 2022. U.S. production, scaled from approximately 14,000 155mm rounds per month in early 2022 to over 40,000 by October 2024, with targets to reach 100,000 per month by late 2025 or 2026, remains constrained by workforce, supply chain, and component limitations even as it represents a nearly threefold increase. Replacement cycles for precision-guided munitions, Patriot interceptors, and air-to-air missiles extend over 18–36 months, while adversary weapons and drones can be produced in weeks. The temporal asymmetry between consumption and replacement introduces operational and strategic constraints that cascade from tactical decision-making to alliance planning assumptions. Commanders adjust operational tempo to conserve scarce munitions, and NATO planners must confront the reality that simultaneous multi-theater commitments may exceed collective industrial capacity.

Furthermore, the geography of production introduces additional vulnerability. Concentrated facilities, whether in Germany, France, or the United States, could themselves be targets of attack or disruption. This creates a strategic risk rarely discussed in public analyses: the industrial base underpinning military capability is not evenly distributed, and its concentration amplifies the consequences of disruption. Civil-military integration, as pursued in China, demonstrates the contrast: Chinese defense planners can leverage civilian industrial capacity rapidly and without the regulatory, workforce, or supply-chain constraints faced by Western nations, highlighting the structural disadvantage inherent in Western industrial organization.

Taken together, these factors illustrate the paradox that defines contemporary Western defense production. Industrial bases optimized for efficiency, quality, and proprietary technological complexity are ill-suited to meet the demands of sustained, high-intensity conflict. Supply chains, labor, regulatory, and financial incentives collectively constrain rapid scaling, creating bottlenecks that are neither apparent in peacetime planning nor easily remedied by additional funding. The Ukraine conflict has revealed these vulnerabilities with unprecedented clarity, demonstrating that operational readiness cannot be assessed solely through platforms and stockpiles but must consider the underlying industrial mathematics of production, human capital, and temporal constraints.

The challenge for Western defense establishments is profound. Rebuilding surge capacity will require addressing regulatory bottlenecks, retraining workforces, diversifying supply chains, and potentially revisiting government ownership or incentive structures for private contractors. Ignoring these structural constraints risks continuing to overestimate NATO's ability to sustain allies in prolonged high-intensity conflicts, with consequences that extend from battlefield outcomes to the credibility of alliance commitments and the fundamental assumptions underlying deterrence. The production paradox is thus not a technical detail of industrial policy; it is a strategic reality that shapes the boundaries of what is militarily possible and what is politically credible in the twenty-first century.

Chapter 3

The New Metrics of Military Power

Traditional assessments of military capability have emphasized platform counts, training readiness levels, and technological sophistication as the primary indicators of military strength. However, the experience of prolonged conflict in Ukraine has demonstrated that these conventional metrics provide incomplete and potentially misleading measures of a nation's ability to sustain military operations against peer adversaries. The emergence of industrial capacity as a decisive factor in military outcomes requires a fundamental reconsideration of how defense establishments evaluate their readiness for sustained operations and allocate resources among competing priorities.

The conventional approach to measuring military power evolved during the Cold War when defense establishments anticipated that any conflict between major powers would be decided within weeks or months through the employment of existing force structures and stockpiled supplies. Under these assumptions, the relevant metrics focused on the immediate capabilities that military forces could bring to bear during the opening phases of conflict: the number of operational aircraft, the readiness rates of ground forces, the size of strategic stockpiles, and the technological sophistication of weapons systems compared to potential adversaries.

These metrics served their intended purpose reasonably well during the limited interventions that characterized post-Cold War military operations. Conflicts in the Balkans, Iraq, Afghanistan, and Libya were indeed decided primarily by the technological superiority and tactical proficiency of Western military forces, with industrial capacity playing a supporting role in sustaining operations over time but rarely becoming a decisive constraint on military outcomes. The apparent success of these operations reinforced confidence in traditional assessments of military capability and provided little incentive to develop alternative metrics.

The Ukraine conflict has revealed the limitations of this approach by demonstrating how industrial capacity can become the binding constraint on military effectiveness even when military forces possess technological advantages and superior training. Ukrainian forces equipped with Western artillery systems and trained by NATO instructors have proven tactically effective against Russian forces, but their operational capabilities have been constrained by the availability of ammunition rather than platform performance or crew proficiency. This dynamic suggests that sustainable military power depends as much on the ability to produce munitions, spare parts, and replacement equipment as on the sophistication of existing systems.

The mathematics of ammunition consumption in sustained conflict provide a stark illustration of this dynamic. Modern artillery systems can fire at rates that would exhaust traditional strategic stockpiles within weeks of continuous operation. A single M777 howitzer can fire up to five rounds per minute during sustained operations, meaning that a typical artillery battery of six howitzers could theoretically consume 43,200 rounds in a single day of continuous operation. While continuous firing at maximum rates is operationally unrealistic, even modest engagement rates can quickly exhaust ammunition supplies that seemed adequate during peacetime planning.

The production rates needed to sustain these consumption levels far exceed the output of Western ammunition manufacturing facilities optimized for peacetime demand. Replacing the ammunition consumed by a single artillery battery during one day of intensive combat would require the entire monthly output of a medium-sized munitions factory. Scaling this calculation to the dozens of artillery battalions that might be involved in a major conflict reveals production requirements that dwarf the current capacity of the Western defense industrial base.

Similar dynamics apply across the spectrum of military consumables, from small arms ammunition to precision-guided missiles to spare parts for complex systems. The Javelin anti-tank missiles that have proven so effective in Ukrainian hands are produced at rates measured in thousands per year, but they can be consumed at rates measured in dozens per day during intensive combat operations. The sophisticated sensors, processors, and guidance systems that make these weapons effective also make them expensive and time-consuming to manufacture, creating inherent tensions between capability and sustainability.

The recognition of industrial capacity as a critical component of military power requires developing new metrics that capture a nation's ability to sustain military operations over extended periods rather than simply its ability to conduct initial operations with existing forces. These metrics must account not only for current production capacity but also for surge potential, supply chain resilience, and the time required to scale production in response to changing requirements.

Manufacturing surge capacity represents a particularly complex measurement challenge because it involves assessing potential capabilities rather than current output levels. A munitions factory operating at fifty percent of its theoretical capacity might appear less capable than one operating at full capacity, but the former actually possesses greater surge potential if it can rapidly increase production by hiring additional workers or extending operating hours. The assessment becomes more complex when considering the time required to implement various scaling options and the sustainability of increased production rates over extended periods.

Supply chain resilience adds another dimension to the assessment of industrial military capacity because modern defense manufacturing depends on components and materials sourced from multiple countries and suppliers. A nation might possess extensive final assembly capacity for military systems while remaining vulnerable to disruption of critical component supplies from foreign sources. The assessment of true industrial military capacity must therefore include analysis of supply chain vulnerabilities and the availability of alternative suppliers for critical components.

The time dimension of industrial capacity assessment presents particular challenges for defense planners accustomed to thinking about military readiness in terms of current capabilities rather than potential future output. The lead times for scaling munitions production can extend for years when new facilities must be constructed or when supply chains must be established for specialized components. These timescales far exceed the planning horizons typically used for military operations, creating mismatches between strategic requirements and industrial realities.

The assessment of industrial military capacity must also account for the broader economic and regulatory environment that shapes production possibilities. Environmental regulations, labor laws, safety requirements, and zoning restrictions all influence the speed and scale with which production can be increased during emergencies. Nations with more flexible regulatory frameworks might possess greater surge potential than those with more restrictive environments, even if their peacetime production levels appear similar.

The human capital dimension of industrial capacity deserves particular attention because skilled manufacturing workers cannot be rapidly trained or easily replaced when production must be scaled quickly. The assessment of true industrial military capacity must therefore include analysis of the available workforce with relevant skills, the capacity of training programs to develop additional skilled workers, and the demographic trends that will affect workforce availability over time.

International comparisons of industrial military capacity reveal significant variations among nations with apparently similar defense capabilities as measured by traditional metrics. China has maintained substantial state-owned munitions manufacturing capacity and has demonstrated the ability to rapidly scale production when needed. Russia entered the Ukraine conflict with extensive ammunition stockpiles and production capacity, though international sanctions have subsequently constrained access to critical components. European nations generally possess sophisticated defense manufacturing capabilities but have optimized for efficiency rather than surge capacity.

The United States presents a particularly complex case because its defense industrial base combines extensive technological capabilities with production capacity that has been optimized for peacetime efficiency rather than wartime surge requirements. American defense contractors can produce the world's most sophisticated military systems, but they have limited capacity to rapidly increase production of basic munitions and consumables. This combination of technological strength and production vulnerability creates strategic risks that traditional assessments of military capability fail to capture adequately.

The implications of industrial capacity as a determinant of military power extend beyond procurement policies to encompass broader questions of strategic planning and alliance relationships. If sustained military operations require industrial surge capacity that few nations possess independently, then alliance partnerships become essential not only for sharing operational burdens but also for providing complementary industrial capabilities. NATO's response to Ukrainian ammunition requirements has effectively created an alliance-wide industrial mobilization that demonstrates both the potential and the limitations of this approach.

The development of new metrics for assessing military power must also consider the interaction between industrial capacity and other factors that influence military effectiveness. Technological sophistication can partially compensate for limited quantities by improving the effectiveness of individual weapons systems. Superior training and tactics can achieve military objectives with fewer resources than would otherwise be required. Intelligence advantages can enable more efficient targeting and reduce ammunition consumption. However, these compensating factors have limits, and prolonged conflicts may eventually exhaust even the most efficiently employed forces.

The challenge facing defense establishments is developing assessment frameworks that integrate traditional measures of military capability with industrial capacity metrics to provide more complete pictures of readiness for sustained operations against peer adversaries. This integration requires sophisticated modeling of how different factors interact under various conflict scenarios and how industrial capacity constraints might affect operational planning and strategic decision-making.

Chapter 4

The Mobilization Impossibility

The prevailing belief that democratic societies can swiftly convert their industrial capacities for military production during international crises, akin to the rapid mobilizations of the World Wars, has become a deeply ingrained yet perilous myth in contemporary defense planning. This assumption forms the bedrock of strategic calculations concerning acceptable peacetime military production levels, assessments of defense industrial readiness, and projections of how democratic alliances would respond to sustained conflicts with peer adversaries. However, the structural transformations that have reshaped advanced economies since 1945 have introduced formidable obstacles to rapid industrial mobilization, challenges that defense establishments have been notably reluctant to confront.

The World War II experience of industrial mobilization has attained an almost mythological status in American and European strategic thinking, offering a compelling narrative about democratic societies' capacity to swiftly reorient their economies in the face of existential threats. The statistics are indeed striking: American aircraft production escalated from fewer than 6,000 planes in 1939 to over 96,000 in 1944, while tank production surged from virtually zero to over 17,000 annually. Similar transformations occurred across the industrial economies of the Allied nations, underscoring the potential for rapid scaling when entire societies commit to military production.

Yet, the economic and regulatory environment that facilitated these transformations has undergone fundamental changes, rendering similar mobilization efforts considerably more challenging under contemporary conditions. These differences transcend mere matters of scale or complexity; they reflect structural changes in how advanced economies are organized, regulated, and operated. Acknowledging these changes is crucial for a realistic assessment of how democratic societies might respond to sustained military conflicts in the twenty-first century.

One of the most significant obstacles to rapid industrial mobilization today is the contemporary environmental regulatory framework. Designed to prevent or minimize industrial activities that might cause ecological damage or public health risks, these regulations encompass most activities associated with large-scale munitions production. The facilities required to manufacture explosives, propellants, and other military supplies inevitably involve processes that generate air emissions, water discharges, and waste products, all of which trigger extensive regulatory review requirements.

The environmental impact assessment processes governing major industrial projects operate on timescales that assume normal commercial planning horizons rather than the urgent demands of military requirements. A typical environmental impact statement for a new munitions manufacturing facility might require two to three years to complete, including public comment periods, agency reviews, and potential legal challenges. Compressing these timescales significantly without compromising the substantive analysis that environmental regulations are designed to ensure is a daunting task.

Moreover, the legal framework surrounding environmental regulations introduces additional obstacles to rapid mobilization. It provides extensive opportunities for public participation and judicial review, which can extend approval processes indefinitely. Environmental groups, local communities, and other stakeholders possess legal rights to challenge industrial projects they believe might cause environmental damage, and courts have consistently upheld these rights, even when national security considerations are involved. The prospect of extended legal battles over new industrial facilities creates powerful disincentives for attempting rapid mobilization efforts.

The transformation of the American workforce since World War II further complicates industrial mobilization efforts. The manufacturing workforce that enabled rapid mobilization during the 1940s was largely composed of semi-skilled workers who could be quickly trained to operate relatively simple production machinery. In contrast, contemporary manufacturing requires significantly higher skill levels and more extensive training periods that cannot be compressed without compromising safety and quality.

Additionally, the demographic composition of the current workforce differs fundamentally from that available during World War II. The entry of women into the workforce during the 1940s provided a large reservoir of potential manufacturing workers who could be rapidly recruited and trained. Today, workforce participation rates are already near historical highs, offering limited additional labor that could be mobilized for defense production without disrupting other essential economic activities.

The geographic distribution of the population has also shifted dramatically since the 1940s, with fewer Americans residing in the industrial regions where defense production would most likely be concentrated. The social and economic disruptions associated with rapidly relocating large numbers of workers to support defense production would be far more severe today than they were during World War II, when the population was more mobile and social support systems were less developed.

Furthermore, the regulatory environment governing workplace safety has evolved in ways that would significantly complicate the rapid expansion of munitions production. Contemporary occupational safety and health regulations are designed to protect workers from industrial hazards that were often overlooked during previous conflicts. While these regulations serve legitimate purposes in safeguarding worker health and safety, they also require extensive training, equipment, and procedural compliance that cannot be implemented rapidly during emergency mobilization efforts.

The financial structure of contemporary corporations presents additional obstacles to rapid mobilization. During World War II, many major industrial firms were privately owned and could make rapid strategic decisions without extensive consultation with shareholders and financial markets. Today, public corporations must consider the interests of shareholders, bondholders, and other financial stakeholders when making major strategic decisions, including those related to defense production.

The legal obligations that corporate managers have to shareholders can conflict with national mobilization requirements if defense production is likely to reduce corporate profitability or expose companies to financial risks. Unlike during World War II, when patriotic duty and government pressure could override financial considerations, contemporary corporate governance structures provide limited mechanisms for prioritizing national security requirements over fiduciary duties to shareholders.

The just-in-time production methods that have become standard throughout American manufacturing represent another fundamental obstacle to rapid mobilization. These methods are designed to minimize inventory costs and maximize efficiency by coordinating production schedules precisely with demand requirements. While just-in-time methods provide significant efficiency advantages during normal operations, they create vulnerabilities during emergency situations when supply chains may be disrupted and demand patterns may change rapidly.

The conversion of civilian production facilities to military use, which provided much of the surge capacity during World War II, would be far more difficult under contemporary conditions due to the specialization that characterizes modern manufacturing. The automobile plants that were converted to aircraft and tank production during the 1940s employed relatively simple manufacturing processes that could be adapted to military production with modest retooling efforts. Today, manufacturing facilities are highly specialized and automated in ways that make conversion to alternative products extremely difficult and expensive.

The information technology systems that control modern manufacturing are typically designed for specific products and processes, making them difficult to reprogram for alternative uses. The skilled technicians needed to operate and maintain these systems are often specialists in particular manufacturing processes who cannot easily adapt to different production requirements. The result is a manufacturing base that achieves high efficiency for its intended purposes but possesses limited flexibility for emergency adaptation.

The international supply chains that support contemporary manufacturing introduce additional vulnerabilities that would severely limit mobilization efforts during international conflicts. Modern defense manufacturing depends on components and materials sourced from numerous foreign suppliers, many of whom are located in countries that might become unavailable during the conflicts that would trigger mobilization requirements. The semiconductors, rare earth elements, specialized chemicals, and precision components essential for contemporary weapons systems cannot be rapidly sourced from alternative suppliers without extensive advance planning.

The financial costs associated with rapid industrial mobilization would be enormous under contemporary conditions due to the regulatory compliance, environmental mitigation, and workforce training requirements that did not exist during previous conflicts. The government financing mechanisms that supported mobilization during World War II were implemented during an era of much simpler regulatory environments and lower environmental standards. Contemporary mobilization efforts would require vastly more complex and expensive approaches to achieve similar results.

The political constraints on mobilization efforts have also evolved in ways that would complicate rapid responses to international crises. The broad public support for mobilization that existed during World War II reflected a national consensus about threat levels and appropriate responses that may not exist during future conflicts. Contemporary democratic societies are more politically polarized and may find it difficult to achieve the consensus necessary for mobilization efforts that would require significant economic disruptions and lifestyle changes.

The media environment has changed in ways that would make mobilization efforts far more difficult to implement and sustain. During World War II, government officials could rely on a relatively small number of media outlets to communicate mobilization requirements and maintain public support. Today, media environments are fragmented and often adversarial toward government initiatives, making it difficult to build and maintain the public consensus that mobilization efforts would require.

These structural obstacles to rapid mobilization do not imply that democratic societies are incapable of increasing defense production during international crises. However, they do suggest that the timescales and scales of increase that might be achievable are far more limited than historical precedents might suggest. Defense planners who assume that mobilization can provide surge capacity comparable to World War II levels are likely to be disappointed when such capacity is actually needed.

The implications of these constraints are profound for strategic planning and force structure decisions. If rapid mobilization cannot provide the surge capacity that strategic plans assume, then peacetime production levels and strategic stockpiles must be sufficient to sustain military operations without relying on rapid increases in production capacity. This realization necessitates a fundamental reconsideration of defense procurement priorities and investment strategies.

Chapter 5
Commercial Supply Chain Vulnerabilities

The integration of commercial supply chains into defense manufacturing has introduced vulnerabilities that extend far beyond traditional military planning, threatening to undermine the industrial foundations of military power in ways that conventional threat assessments have failed to anticipate adequately. These vulnerabilities arise not from deliberate attacks on military facilities or supply lines but from the complex interdependencies that characterize modern global manufacturing networks and the civilian economic systems that support them.

The semiconductor industry provides the most visible and consequential example of how commercial supply chain vulnerabilities can affect military capabilities. Modern weapons systems depend on electronic components that are manufactured using the same facilities, materials, and supply chains that support civilian electronics production. The sophisticated processors that enable precision guidance in military missiles are produced in the same fabrication facilities that manufacture chips for smartphones and computers. The sensors that provide target identification capabilities in military systems use semiconductor technologies developed primarily for commercial markets.

This integration creates dependencies that extend throughout the defense supply base in ways that are often invisible to military planners focused on immediate procurement requirements rather than underlying supply chain structures. A disruption in semiconductor production that primarily affects civilian markets will inevitably affect military production as well, but the military impact may not become apparent until months after the initial disruption occurs. The long lead times associated with military procurement can obscure these dependencies until they become critical constraints on operational capabilities.

The geographic concentration of semiconductor manufacturing in East Asia creates particular strategic risks for Western militaries that depend on reliable access to advanced electronic components. The Taiwan Semiconductor Manufacturing Company (TSMC) produces over half of the world's semiconductors and an even higher percentage of the most advanced chips used in military systems. A disruption of TSMC's operations, whether due to natural disasters, political instability, or military conflict, would severely constrain the production of new military systems and the maintenance of existing ones.

The technical complexity of semiconductor manufacturing means that alternative production sources cannot be rapidly established if primary suppliers become unavailable. Modern fabrication facilities require investments measured in tens of billions of dollars and several years of construction time before they can begin production. The specialized equipment used in these facilities is itself produced by a small number of suppliers, creating additional bottlenecks that would delay any efforts to establish alternative production capacity.

The materials used in semiconductor manufacturing create another layer of supply chain vulnerability. The ultra-pure silicon wafers that serve as the foundation for all semiconductor devices are produced by a handful of companies located primarily in Asia. The specialized chemicals used in the etching and cleaning processes that create circuit patterns on these wafers come from an even smaller number of suppliers. The rare gases used in various manufacturing steps are often available from only one or two sources worldwide.

These material dependencies extend beyond the semiconductor industry to encompass virtually every component of modern military systems. The rare earth elements used in permanent magnets for electric motors and generators are dominated by Chinese sources that control over eighty percent of global production. The lithium used in batteries for portable military equipment comes primarily from mines in Chile, Australia, and China. The cobalt used in high-performance alloys comes largely from the Democratic Republic of Congo, where political instability and ethical concerns about mining practices create additional supply risks.

The concentration of raw material production in politically unstable regions or potentially hostile nations creates strategic vulnerabilities that go beyond simple supply interruption. Nations that control critical materials can use that control as political leverage, threatening to restrict supplies unless political or military concessions are made. The European experience with Russian natural gas provides a dramatic illustration of how resource dependencies can become tools of political coercion.

The manufacturing processes that transform raw materials into components for military systems often exhibit similar geographic concentration patterns that create additional vulnerabilities. The specialized steel alloys used in military applications are produced by a relatively small number of steel companies that have invested in the equipment and expertise needed to meet military specifications. The precision machining capabilities needed to produce complex mechanical components are concentrated in industrial regions that might be vulnerable to various forms of disruption.

The transportation networks that connect these geographically dispersed supply chains create another layer of vulnerability that has become increasingly apparent as global trade has grown more complex and interconnected. Modern supply chains depend on reliable access to shipping, aviation, and ground transportation networks that can be disrupted by natural disasters, labor disputes, terrorist attacks, or military action. The disruptions caused by the Ever Given container ship blocking the Suez Canal in 2021 demonstrated how single points of failure in transportation networks can affect global supply chains for weeks or months.

The information systems that coordinate these complex supply networks represent an additional vulnerability that is often overlooked in traditional assessments of supply chain risks. Modern supply chains depend on sophisticated software systems that track inventory levels, coordinate production schedules, and manage financial transactions across multiple companies and countries. Cyberattacks on these systems could disrupt supply chains without causing any physical damage to manufacturing facilities or transportation networks.

The financial systems that support international trade create yet another layer of vulnerability that could affect defense supply chains during international crises. The banking networks that process payments for international transactions, the insurance companies that cover transportation risks, and the credit systems that finance inventory purchases all represent potential points of failure that could disrupt supply chains even if physical manufacturing and transportation capacity remains intact.

The interconnected nature of these vulnerabilities means that disruptions can cascade through supply networks in ways that amplify their ultimate impact on military production. A natural disaster that disrupts semiconductor production in Asia might force civilian electronics manufacturers to compete more aggressively for available supplies, driving up prices and extending delivery times for military electronics. A cyberattack on shipping coordination systems might create transportation bottlenecks that affect multiple industries simultaneously. A financial crisis that constrains credit availability might force suppliers to prioritize customers who can pay immediately over those with longer payment terms.

The time dimensions of supply chain vulnerabilities create particular challenges for military planners accustomed to thinking about threats in terms of immediate risks rather than gradual degradation of capabilities. Supply chain disruptions typically do not cause immediate failures of military systems but instead create gradually increasing constraints on maintenance, upgrades, and new production. These gradual effects can be difficult to detect and even harder to address once they become apparent.

The commercial optimization of supply chains for efficiency rather than resilience has eliminated much of the redundancy that might otherwise provide protection against disruptions. Just-in-time manufacturing practices have reduced inventory levels throughout supply networks, meaning that even brief disruptions can quickly exhaust available supplies. Single-sourcing arrangements that provide cost savings during normal operations become critical vulnerabilities when primary suppliers become unavailable.

The global nature of modern supply chains means that military establishments have limited visibility into the full extent of their supply dependencies. Prime contractors typically focus on their immediate supplier relationships and may not have comprehensive knowledge of the sub-suppliers, raw material sources, and manufacturing processes that ultimately support their production. This lack of visibility means that military planners may not discover critical vulnerabilities until they are exposed by actual disruptions.

The complexity of modern supply chains has grown to the point where even sophisticated companies struggle to map their complete supplier networks. A single military system might incorporate components from dozens of primary suppliers, each of whom depends on hundreds of their own suppliers, creating supply networks that extend through multiple tiers and cross numerous national boundaries. The computational challenges of tracking all these relationships exceed the capabilities of most organizations, leaving significant blind spots in supply chain risk assessment.

The commercial incentives that drive supply chain decisions often conflict with military requirements for reliability and security. Commercial suppliers optimize for cost reduction, delivery speed, and flexibility rather than for the redundancy and security that military applications might require. These optimization decisions are made independently by each participant in the supply chain based on their own financial interests rather than broader considerations about national security implications.

The pharmaceutical industry provides another instructive example of how commercial supply chain vulnerabilities can affect military capabilities. Military medical supplies depend heavily on the same manufacturing facilities and supply chains that support civilian healthcare. The active pharmaceutical ingredients used in military medications are often produced in the same facilities that manufacture civilian drugs, using raw materials sourced from the same suppliers.

The geographic concentration of pharmaceutical manufacturing has created strategic vulnerabilities that became apparent during the COVID-19 pandemic when supply chain disruptions affected the availability of basic medical supplies and medications. China and India together control significant portions of global pharmaceutical production, including many medications that are essential for military medical support. A disruption in these supply chains during a conflict involving these nations could severely compromise military medical capabilities.

The regulatory frameworks that govern pharmaceutical manufacturing create additional complexities for addressing supply chain vulnerabilities. Military medical supplies must meet the same safety and efficacy standards that apply to civilian medications, which means that alternative suppliers cannot be qualified rapidly if primary sources become unavailable. The clinical testing and regulatory approval processes required for new suppliers can take years to complete, making it extremely difficult to respond quickly to supply chain disruptions.

The aerospace industry exhibits supply chain characteristics that create particular vulnerabilities for military aviation capabilities. Modern military aircraft incorporate components from thousands of suppliers located throughout the global economy. The specialized materials used in jet engines, the advanced composites used in airframes, and the sophisticated electronics used in avionics systems all depend on supply chains that serve both military and civilian

Chapter 6

The Drone Revolution and Asymmetric Manufacturing

The evolution of unmanned aerial systems (UAS) in the Ukraine conflict has not only redefined tactical engagements but has also catalyzed a paradigm shift in the economics and logistics of modern warfare. This transformation underscores a broader reimagining of military capability development, procurement, and deployment, challenging entrenched doctrines that have long equated technological sophistication with military effectiveness.

In the face of a technologically superior adversary, Ukrainian forces have leveraged commercially available drones, such as the DJI Mavic 3, to execute operations traditionally reserved for high-end military hardware. These drones, often costing a few hundred dollars, have been adapted with explosive payloads to engage targets like Russian main battle tanks and artillery systems, which are valued in the millions. This inversion of the traditional cost-exchange ratio, where a low-cost drone disables a high-value target, has profound implications for military budgeting and procurement strategies.

The mathematical implications of these engagements are stark. A drone costing $500 that successfully disables a $5 million tank represents a cost-exchange ratio of 10,000:1 in favor of the attacking force. Even accounting for variables such as engagement probability and operational sustainability, these ratios suggest that traditional approaches to military capability development may be fundamentally unsuitable for conflicts where adversaries can employ mass-produced, expendable systems.

This shift is not merely tactical but extends to the very nature of military manufacturing. Commercial drone manufacturers have optimized their production systems for high-volume, low-cost manufacturing using readily available components and automated assembly processes. These manufacturing approaches can rapidly scale production in response to increased demand without requiring the specialized facilities, security clearances, or regulatory approvals that constrain traditional military manufacturing. The component supply chains that support commercial drone production demonstrate how civilian technologies can be rapidly militarized without requiring traditional defense industrial conversion processes.

The software dimensions of drone militarization present particular challenges for traditional approaches to military technology development and export control. The artificial intelligence algorithms that enable autonomous flight, target recognition, and navigation can be developed using commercially available programming tools and computing resources. The open-source nature of much software development means that military-capable algorithms can be shared rapidly among diverse actors without requiring formal technology transfer agreements or export licenses.

The rapid evolution of commercial drone technologies creates a dynamic competitive environment that differs fundamentally from traditional military technology development cycles. Commercial drone manufacturers introduce new models and capabilities on timescales measured in months rather than the years or decades that characterize military system development. This rapid pace of commercial innovation makes it difficult for traditional military acquisition processes to keep pace with evolving capabilities and threats.

The Ukrainian experience has demonstrated how commercial drone technologies can be rapidly adapted for military purposes through modifications that require minimal specialized knowledge or equipment. The addition of explosive charges, improved communication systems, or enhanced sensors can transform civilian drones into effective military systems without requiring fundamental redesign or specialized manufacturing processes. These modifications can be implemented by small teams with limited resources rather than major defense contractors with extensive facilities.

The manufacturing scalability of drone systems creates strategic implications that extend beyond their immediate military applications. Unlike traditional military systems that require specialized production facilities and long lead times, drone systems can potentially be manufactured using civilian industrial capacity that could be rapidly converted to military production during conflicts. This manufacturing flexibility creates surge production potential that traditional military systems typically cannot match.

The distributed manufacturing possibilities enabled by drone technologies represent a fundamental departure from the centralized production approaches that have characterized military manufacturing since World War II. Small teams with access to commercial components and basic manufacturing equipment can potentially produce military-effective drone systems without requiring access to major industrial facilities or sophisticated supply chains.

The implications of distributed drone manufacturing for strategic stability and conflict dynamics deserve careful analysis because they suggest that traditional approaches to controlling military technology proliferation may be inadequate for addressing drone-enabled threats. Export controls that focus on complete weapons systems or specialized military components may be ineffective when military capabilities can be assembled from commercially available components using widely available technical knowledge.

The defensive challenges posed by mass drone employment have proven particularly difficult for traditional air defense systems designed to engage high-value targets with sophisticated countermeasures. The radar signatures, flight patterns, and electronic characteristics of small commercial drones often differ significantly from traditional aircraft threats, making them difficult to detect and track using conventional air defense sensors.

The economic calculations underlying air defense against drone swarms reveal fundamental mismatches between defensive costs and offensive costs that favor attacking forces employing large numbers of inexpensive systems. Traditional surface-to-air missiles that cost hundreds of thousands or millions of dollars each are poorly suited for engaging drone targets that cost orders of magnitude less. The mathematics of such exchanges strongly favor the attacking force and could rapidly exhaust defensive missile inventories.

The development of cost-effective drone defense systems has proven challenging because it requires fundamentally different technical approaches than those used for traditional air defense. Directed energy weapons, electronic warfare systems, and kinetic interceptors designed specifically for drone threats represent promising approaches, but they require significant development efforts and manufacturing investments that may not be immediately available.

The integration of artificial intelligence into drone systems creates additional challenges for defensive planning because it enables autonomous behavior that does not require continuous communication with operators. AI-enabled drones can potentially operate in contested electromagnetic environments where traditional remotely piloted systems would be ineffective. The decision-making capabilities provided by AI systems enable drone swarms to adapt their tactics dynamically in response to defensive measures.

The proliferation of AI-enabled drone technologies raises profound questions about the future character of warfare and the role of human decision-making in military operations. Autonomous weapons systems that can select and engage targets without human intervention represent a fundamental departure from traditional military doctrine and raise significant legal, ethical, and strategic concerns that defense establishments are only beginning to address systematically.

The manufacturing implications of AI-enabled drone systems extend beyond hardware production to encompass software development and algorithm training processes that differ fundamentally from traditional military technology development. AI algorithms can be developed and refined using commercial computing resources and public datasets, making them accessible to a much broader range of potential military actors than traditional weapons technologies.

The international implications of drone proliferation and distributed manufacturing deserve particular attention because they suggest that military capabilities that were previously available only to major powers may become accessible to smaller nations, non-state actors, and criminal organizations. This democratization of military technology could fundamentally alter regional power balances and create new categories of security threats that existing international agreements and institutions are not designed to address.

The response strategies available to traditional military establishments faced with these emerging capabilities require fundamental reconsideration of force structures, operational concepts, and acquisition priorities. The emphasis on high-cost, sophisticated platforms that has characterized Western military development may need to shift toward approaches that can address mass, low-cost threats more effectively.

In summary, the drone revolution in warfare is not merely a technological innovation but a comprehensive transformation that challenges existing paradigms of military strategy, manufacturing, and defense policy. As adversaries increasingly exploit the accessibility and adaptability of commercial technologies, traditional military establishments must adapt to maintain strategic relevance in an era of asymmetric warfare.

Chapter 7

Strategic Implications and the Future of Military Power

The convergence of industrial capacity constraints, supply chain vulnerabilities, and technological disruption has created a strategic environment that challenges fundamental assumptions about how military power is generated, sustained, and employed in international competition. The implications of these changes extend far beyond procurement policies and tactical applications to encompass broader questions about alliance relationships, deterrence strategies, and the balance of power among major nations.

The recognition that industrial capacity has become a decisive factor in military effectiveness requires fundamental reconsideration of how nations assess their strategic position relative to potential adversaries. Traditional measures of military power that emphasized platform counts, technological sophistication, and training readiness provide incomplete pictures of national military capability when prolonged conflicts require sustained production of munitions and replacement equipment at scales that exceed peacetime manufacturing capacity.

China's approach to maintaining military-industrial capacity offers a particularly instructive contrast to Western practices and demonstrates how different strategic cultures and economic systems can produce fundamentally different approaches to military preparedness. Chinese military doctrine has consistently emphasized the importance of "People's War" concepts that assume prolonged conflicts requiring mobilization of entire societies and economies. This doctrinal emphasis has translated into industrial policies that maintain surge production capacity even when peacetime demand would not justify such investments.

The Chinese defense industry operates under fundamentally different economic constraints than Western defense contractors because state ownership and strategic direction can override market-based calculations about optimal capacity utilization. Chinese aerospace manufacturers, shipbuilders, and munitions producers maintain production capacity that exceeds current military requirements but provides surge potential that could be rapidly activated during conflicts. This approach represents a strategic investment in industrial preparedness that Western market-based systems have found difficult to justify financially.

The implications of these different approaches to defense industrial capacity become apparent when considering scenarios for prolonged conflicts between major powers. Western militaries that have optimized their force structures and procurement strategies for rapid, decisive operations may find themselves at significant disadvantages during conflicts that extend beyond their initial stockpiles and surge production capabilities. The mathematical reality of consumption rates versus production rates could create strategic vulnerabilities that traditional assessments of military balance have failed to anticipate adequately.

Russian performance in the Ukraine conflict provides additional insights into how industrial capacity affects strategic outcomes during prolonged conflicts. Despite suffering significant military setbacks and facing extensive international sanctions, Russia has demonstrated the ability to sustain military operations through domestic production capacity and alternative supply chains that Western intelligence services appear to have underestimated. The resilience of Russian military production under adverse conditions suggests that Western assumptions about the fragility of adversary industrial bases may require significant revision.

The sanctions imposed on Russia have created a natural experiment in supply chain resilience that offers valuable lessons for understanding how modern economies respond to attempts to disrupt their defense industrial capacity. Russian adaptation to sanctions has involved developing alternative supply chains, increasing domestic production capacity, and establishing new partnerships with nations willing to provide critical components and materials. The effectiveness of these adaptations has implications for how sanctions might be expected to affect other potential adversaries and for how nations might prepare their own industrial bases for similar pressures.

The alliance implications of industrial capacity as a determinant of military effectiveness deserve particular attention because they suggest that traditional approaches to burden-sharing and interoperability may be inadequate for conflicts that require sustained high-intensity operations. NATO's response to Ukrainian ammunition requirements has demonstrated both the potential benefits of allied industrial cooperation and the limitations of current alliance industrial capacity when faced with major conflict requirements.

The geographic distribution of defense industrial capacity within NATO reveals significant vulnerabilities that could affect alliance effectiveness during major conflicts. European nations possess sophisticated defense manufacturing capabilities but have generally optimized for efficiency rather than surge capacity. The United States maintains broader defense industrial capacity but faces its own constraints in scaling production rapidly. The result is an alliance industrial base that might struggle to sustain multiple simultaneous major operations against peer adversaries.

The development of alliance industrial strategies that address these vulnerabilities requires coordination mechanisms that extend far beyond traditional military cooperation agreements. Industrial capacity planning involves economic policies, regulatory frameworks, and investment decisions that are typically considered domestic rather than alliance matters. The integration of industrial capacity planning into alliance strategy represents a fundamental expansion of alliance coordination requirements that existing institutions and agreements may not be designed to accommodate.

The technological disruption represented by drone proliferation and distributed manufacturing creates additional strategic implications that challenge traditional approaches to arms control, technology transfer, and conflict escalation management. The democratization of military technology enabled by commercial supply chains and accessible manufacturing processes suggests that military capabilities that were previously available only to major powers may become widely accessible to smaller nations, non-state actors, and criminal organizations.

The arms control implications of these technological changes are profound because existing agreements and institutions are designed to address threats posed by sophisticated weapons systems that require specialized knowledge, materials, and facilities to produce. Drone technologies that can be assembled from commercial components using widely available technical knowledge may be essentially impossible to control through traditional arms control mechanisms that focus on restricting access to specialized military technologies.

The deterrence implications of distributed manufacturing and asymmetric warfare capabilities require careful analysis because they suggest that traditional concepts of escalation control and strategic stability may need fundamental revision. Adversaries who can rapidly scale production of low-cost, high-impact systems may be able to impose costs on traditional military forces that exceed the defender's ability to absorb losses and replace equipment.

The strategic implications of cost-exchange ratios that favor mass-produced, expendable systems over sophisticated, expensive platforms challenge fundamental assumptions about how military effectiveness translates into political outcomes. Military forces that achieve tactical success through technological superiority may find their strategic position undermined by adversaries who can sustain higher loss rates while imposing unsustainable replacement costs on more sophisticated forces.

The information warfare dimensions of contemporary conflicts create additional strategic implications that interact with industrial capacity constraints in complex ways. The ability to wage effective information campaigns may depend as much on industrial capacity to produce communication systems, sensors, and processing equipment as on the sophistication of individual information warfare platforms. Nations with greater capacity to rapidly produce and deploy information warfare systems may gain decisive advantages in shaping public opinion and political outcomes during conflicts.

The cyber warfare implications of supply chain vulnerabilities and distributed manufacturing deserve particular attention because they suggest that traditional concepts of geographic security may be inadequate for protecting critical military capabilities. Cyber attacks on commercial supply chains or manufacturing facilities could affect military capabilities without directly targeting military installations or systems. The attribution challenges associated with such attacks could complicate deterrence strategies and escalation management during international crises.

The economic warfare potential inherent in supply chain vulnerabilities creates strategic implications that extend beyond traditional military considerations to encompass broader questions about economic security and national resilience. Nations that can disrupt adversary supply chains while protecting their own may be able to achieve strategic objectives without engaging in traditional military operations. This potential for economic coercion through supply chain manipulation represents a form of strategic competition that existing international institutions and legal frameworks are not designed to address adequately.

The long-term implications of these strategic changes suggest that the international system may be entering a period of fundamental transformation in how military power is generated, deployed, and employed for political purposes. The assumptions that have guided strategic planning, alliance relationships, and arms control agreements since the end of the Cold War may require comprehensive revision to address the realities of industrial capacity as a determinant of military effectiveness.

The policy responses available to address these strategic challenges require coordination across multiple domains that have traditionally been managed separately: defense procurement, industrial policy, alliance relationships, technology policy, and economic security strategy. The integration of these policy domains into coherent national strategies represents a significant challenge for governments accustomed to managing these issues through separate bureaucratic structures and decision-making processes.

The implications for democratic societies are particularly complex because the policy responses needed to address industrial capacity vulnerabilities may require approaches that conflict with established principles about market efficiency, regulatory frameworks, and international economic integration. The maintenance of surge manufacturing capacity may require government investments and interventions in markets that would be difficult to justify under normal economic criteria but that may be essential for national security.

The time horizons required for addressing these strategic challenges extend far beyond typical political planning cycles, creating additional complications for democratic policy-making processes. The industrial capacity investments needed to address current vulnerabilities may require sustained commitments over decades, while the political benefits of such investments may not become apparent until they are actually needed during international crises that may never occur.

The international coordination required to address supply chain vulnerabilities and develop distributed manufacturing capabilities may require new forms of cooperation among democratic allies that extend beyond traditional military alliance structures. These new forms of cooperation may need to encompass industrial policy, technology development, supply chain management, and regulatory harmonization in ways that represent significant expansions of traditional alliance coordination mechanisms.

The ultimate question raised by this analysis is whether democratic societies possess the institutional capabilities and political will necessary to address the strategic challenges identified in this examination of contemporary military power. The answer to this question will likely determine whether democratic nations maintain their military advantages in an international system where industrial capacity increasingly determines strategic outcomes.

Chapter 8

The Hidden Mathematics of Allied Burden

The public accounting of Western military assistance to Ukraine has systematically obscured the mathematical relationship between consumption rates and production capacity that ultimately determines whether allied industrial systems can sustain prolonged, high-intensity conflicts. Official statistics emphasizing cumulative aid totals and platform deliveries often provide misleading impressions of Western industrial capacity by focusing on absolute numbers rather than the production rates and replacement timelines that govern strategic sustainability. In an era where adversaries can rapidly scale low-cost, high-impact technologies such as drones, precision munitions, and autonomous systems, these distortions are no longer trivial; they represent fundamental blind spots in Western strategic planning.

The European Union's ammunition plan for Ukraine, announced in March 2023, provides a concrete illustration of how political commitments diverge from production mathematics in ways that reveal structural constraints on Western industrial capacity. EU member states agreed to jointly procure one million artillery rounds for delivery within twelve months, with broader commitments to increase production to two million rounds annually by 2025. The initial delivery timeline proved optimistic: by late 2023, only 300,000 rounds had been delivered from existing stockpiles, with an additional 180,000 ordered from manufacturers. However, the EU demonstrated genuine industrial mobilization over the subsequent year. By December 2024, the EU had delivered one million shells, fulfilling its initial pledge roughly nine months behind schedule. By early 2025, deliveries approached the two million shell target, demonstrating both the feasibility of significant production increases and the extended timelines inherent in scaling defense manufacturing.

Yet even this substantial achievement illustrates the fundamental constraint. The mathematics underlying these delivery rates become particularly stark when compared to documented Ukrainian consumption during periods of intensive combat in 2022. Open-source reporting indicates that Ukrainian artillery forces consumed between 6,000 and 8,000 rounds per day at peak periods, rates that would exhaust the EU's annual target of two million rounds in 250 to 333 days of sustained operations. Even the achieved production rate of approximately two million rounds over twelve months provides only 5,480 rounds per day on average, covering 68–91 percent of peak 2022 consumption. More tellingly, by May 2025, Ukraine was receiving approximately 3,700 shells per day from the EU, and the fire ratio stood at 1:3, with Ukraine firing one round for every three Russian shells. These numbers reveal that even achieving stated production goals remains insufficient to match adversary output or restore Ukrainian artillery parity, forcing operational adjustments and tactical constraints directly attributable to industrial capacity limitations.

This discrepancy exposes a structural mismatch between Western industrial systems optimized for efficiency and adversaries whose defense industries prioritize surge capacity. Russian domestic production was estimated at approximately 2.3 million shells in 2024, but Russia's ability to fire up to 7 million rounds that year relied heavily on North Korean supplies, which comprised over 50 percent of monthly Russian consumption by mid-2024. Intelligence assessments indicate North Korea supplied between 3 million and 8 million artillery shells to Russia between 2023 and 2025. While this reveals Russian dependency on external suppliers, the combined Russia-North Korea production and supply network still significantly outpaces NATO collective output. Russian and Chinese production models, informed by decades of planning for sustained conflict, maintain excess capacity, simplified supply chains, and vertical integration that allow rapid mobilization without the bureaucratic overhead that constrains Western manufacturing. The Ukrainian case study underscores that even the most ambitious EU or NATO production targets remain dwarfed by adversary production rates, creating asymmetric consumption-to-production ratios that have strategic significance far beyond immediate tactical outcomes.

Beyond conventional ammunition, the integration of emerging technologies further compounds the burden on Western industrial capacity. AI-enabled drones, autonomous vehicles, and precision-guided munitions introduce layers of complexity because their production depends not only on physical materials but also on software development, testing, and skilled labor capable of integrating algorithms with hardware. Unlike artillery shells or missiles, these systems require continuous iteration, calibration, and quality assurance that cannot be accelerated simply by adding funds. The rapid proliferation of commercial drone technologies and accessible AI software amplifies the mathematical asymmetry, allowing adversaries to scale capabilities in ways that Western production paradigms are ill-equipped to match.

The temporal dimension of industrial asymmetry is particularly critical. While adversaries like Russia, even relying partly on North Korean supplies, can collectively produce in ninety to one hundred twenty days what NATO produces in 365, Western military production schedules for advanced systems often extend across multiple years. Long-range precision strike weapons, advanced interceptors, and next-generation aircraft require production cycles measured in months to years, yet are consumed within hours or days of deployment. The mismatch between consumption and replacement timelines creates operational feedback loops: commanders must ration resources, prioritize engagement, and adjust tactics to preserve limited stockpiles, embedding industrial constraints directly into battlefield decision-making.

Human capital represents another absolute limit on surge capacity. Skilled machinists, foundry workers, precision assemblers, and technicians form the backbone of defense production. The pipeline for training such personnel spans years, and workforce demographics in Europe and the United States indicate long-term shortfalls in these critical skills. Apprenticeship programs, on-the-job experience, and specialized training cannot be accelerated without eroding quality or safety standards, meaning that even if raw materials and production facilities were available, the bottleneck created by human capital remains insurmountable in the near term. Security clearance requirements exacerbate this problem. In the United States alone, hundreds of thousands of pending investigations constrain the rapid expansion of cleared workforces, creating a legal and bureaucratic ceiling on production that cannot be bypassed without fundamental policy changes.

Supply chain vulnerabilities further magnify the strategic burden. Rare earth elements, semiconductors, and specialty steels essential for precision munitions, electronics, and advanced weaponry flow through global networks often dominated by China, which controls roughly 80 percent of processed rare earth output and significant portions of semiconductor supply chains. Taiwan Semiconductor Manufacturing Company (TSMC), which controls over 90 percent of advanced node production (below 10 nanometers), represents a critical single point of failure for Western defense electronics. Western dependence on these supply chains introduces strategic risk: cyberattacks, economic coercion, or geopolitical disruptions could delay production, reduce quality, or raise costs, compounding the industrial asymmetry. This dynamic creates a paradox in which Western military buildup relies on the cooperation of potential adversaries, giving them leverage over timelines, costs, and even tactical effectiveness.

The geographic concentration of critical production facilities adds another layer of vulnerability. European ammunition production is clustered in a limited number of sites, which could become targets for long-range strikes in a conflict scenario. Unlike adversaries whose industrial systems are deliberately dispersed to minimize disruption, Western facilities optimized for efficiency rather than surge capacity present single points of failure. Redundancy, long treated as unnecessary overhead, has been sacrificed in favor of lean, cost-effective operations, leaving allies exposed to cascading production shortfalls in the event of simultaneous crises.

Policy frameworks, accounting methods, and political narratives compound these structural limitations. Equipment transfers to Ukraine are typically valued at depreciated book costs, masking the true replacement burden. A Patriot battery accounted at $400 million may require $1.1 billion and nearly two years to replace under current production schedules, a discrepancy invisible in public accounting yet critical for strategic planning. Precision-guided munitions and advanced interceptors, similarly valued at historical costs, require vastly more industrial capacity to replace in the real world. These accounting distortions, while politically convenient, hide the full strategic implications of ongoing commitments and risk creating a false sense of security among decision-makers and the public.

The asymmetry between Western industrial capacity and adversary production scales has profound consequences for alliance planning, deterrence, and operational doctrine. Every artillery shell, interceptor, or drone deployed to Ukraine represents one less unit available for potential contingencies in the Baltics, Taiwan, or the Indo-Pacific. The cumulative effect of sustained commitments creates path dependence: today's choices lock in constraints on future operational flexibility, reducing strategic options and altering the credibility of deterrence frameworks. Allies must recognize that high consumption rates in one theater can cascade into vulnerabilities in another, forcing political and military planners to make previously unthinkable trade-offs between competing obligations.

China's Military-Civil Fusion strategy illustrates how institutional organization can decisively alter industrial outcomes. By integrating civilian commercial capacity with military production objectives, China eliminates the regulatory, bureaucratic, and security barriers that constrain Western surge capacity. Civilian electronics manufacturers, chemical plants, and precision machining facilities can be redirected for military purposes almost immediately, creating a flexibility Western systems cannot replicate. The contrast between Western compartmentalized industrial structures and China's integrated model highlights the deeper strategic asymmetry: it is not merely production scale but systemic organization that determines the ability to sustain prolonged high-intensity competition.

The implications extend beyond physical production to strategic psychology. Wars in the twenty-first century are increasingly won not solely through attrition of adversary forces but by eroding confidence in industrial sustainability. Even without achieving permanent superiority, adversaries can leverage persistent output advantages and public perception to undermine political will. Russia's ability to sustain operations through a combination of domestic production and North Korean supplies, and China's potential to rapidly mobilize civilian industrial capacity, need not translate into absolute dominance; it is sufficient that their production rates outpace Western replenishment long enough to instill recognition of mathematical impossibility in democratic systems. Once perception of industrial insufficiency takes hold, public and political support for sustained strategic competition can collapse before battlefield outcomes are fully realized.

Finally, the Ukrainian experience underscores that these constraints are not theoretical but empirical. Western assumptions of rapid, decisive victory supported by technological superiority are increasingly incompatible with the realities of contemporary industrial mathematics. The combined effect of production bottlenecks, human capital limitations, supply chain dependencies, emerging technology demands, and temporal asymmetries ensures that Western military capabilities are finite, slow to replenish, and vulnerable to strategic manipulation. This recognition demands a comprehensive reassessment of alliance doctrine, procurement planning, and industrial policy, acknowledging that strategic advantage depends as much on the sustainability of production as on battlefield performance.

The hidden mathematics of allied burden, where consumption rates, production capacity, human capital, and technological integration intersect, defines the strategic landscape of modern warfare. Understanding these relationships is no longer optional; it is a prerequisite for preserving deterrence credibility, sustaining alliance commitments, and maintaining operational flexibility against adversaries who have internalized these lessons over decades. The Ukraine conflict has demonstrated with mathematical clarity that industrial capacity is not merely a supporting factor in military strategy, it is the central determinant of strategic possibility in the twenty-first century.

Chapter 9

The Bureaucratic Bottleneck

When Industrial Dysfunction Meets Strategic Necessity

The mathematical constraints on Western ammunition production documented in preceding chapters represent only one dimension of the industrial capacity crisis confronting democratic military establishments. Equally consequential, though far less visible to public scrutiny, are the organizational pathologies and bureaucratic dysfunctions that compound these limitations. These structural deficiencies, documented in the government's own internal audits and oversight reports, reveal that even modest attempts to scale production encounter obstacles that have little to do with technical capability or financial resources. Instead, they reflect decades of institutional drift, unclear lines of authority, and the erosion of organizational memory regarding surge manufacturing requirements.

A comprehensive examination of U.S. Government Accountability Office (GAO) reports on ammunition procurement and production reveals a pattern of systemic dysfunction that persists despite repeated identification and recommendations for reform. These are not theoretical concerns raised by external critics but empirical findings documented by Congress's investigative arm based on extensive reviews of governing documents, contract structures, and interviews with officials at every level of the ammunition enterprise. The implications extend far beyond administrative inefficiency: when organizational confusion and bureaucratic inertia constrain the ability to rapidly scale production, the result is strategic vulnerability that adversaries can exploit regardless of nominal economic or technological advantages.

The Army's management of ammunition procurement and production involves a complex web of overlapping authorities, intersecting responsibilities, and unclear hierarchies that government auditors have repeatedly identified as impediments to effective operations. The organizational structure that emerged over decades of incremental adjustments lacks the clarity and coherence necessary for rapid decision-making during crises. Multiple Army organizations, Joint Program Executive Office Armaments and Ammunition, Joint Munitions Command, Army Contracting Command, and Combat Capabilities Development Command Armaments Center, share responsibilities for contracts, modernization, life-cycle management, and quality control in ways that create ambiguity about who holds decision authority for critical functions.

This complexity is not accidental but rather the accumulated result of organizational changes that were never fully integrated into governing documents. The creation of Army Futures Command in 2018, for example, transferred research and development responsibilities from Army Materiel Command without corresponding revisions to the memoranda of understanding that delineate roles and responsibilities among ammunition management organizations. Similarly, the 2004 Industrial Base Support Agreement that assigns responsibilities between program offices and munitions commands has not been revised in nearly two decades, despite fundamental changes in organizational structure, mission priorities, and operational requirements. The 2015 Single Manager for Conventional Ammunition Charter references offices that were subsequently dissolved and uses organizational names that were changed years ago.

The consequences of this organizational drift became apparent during government audits of ammunition plant operations. Officials at multiple plants reported lacking clarity about roles and responsibilities due to outdated documentation. Headquarters officials acknowledged that no recent formal documentation outlines current relationships between key organizations responsible for ammunition management. When asked about governing documents, officials described them as "not representative of how the Army currently manages ammunition procurement and production." This gap between formal authority structures and actual operating practices creates an environment where coordination depends on personal relationships and institutional memory rather than clear procedural guidelines, a situation that becomes particularly problematic during personnel transitions or rapid scaling requirements.

The organizational confusion extends to the plant level, where government oversight personnel, contracting officers, quality assurance staff, and vendor employees must navigate overlapping authorities without clear delineation of decision-making power. Government auditors found that only one of five ammunition plants had current formal documentation governing roles and responsibilities at the facility level. At another plant, officials took the initiative to develop an informal document to resolve gaps and overlaps, but this effort was not replicated systematically across other facilities. The result is an environment where critical decisions about facility maintenance, modernization priorities, and contract requirements can be delayed or mishandled due to uncertainty about which organization has authority to act.

The dysfunction in organizational relationships has direct consequences for the modernization efforts that are essential for maintaining and expanding production capacity. Ammunition plants require continuous investment in facility upgrades, equipment replacement, and process improvements to maintain operational capability and respond to changing requirements. Yet the management of modernization projects reveals coordination failures that waste resources and delay capability improvements at precisely the moment when surge capacity is most urgently needed.

The process for approving and executing modernization projects involves multiple organizations with intersecting but poorly defined responsibilities. Joint Program Executive Office Armaments and Ammunition holds decision authority over acquisition strategy and provides funding. Joint Munitions Command submits priority project lists and executes approved projects. Combat Capabilities Development Command Armaments Center provides technical support and project design. Army Contracting Command modifies contracts to incorporate approved projects. This distribution of responsibilities, while theoretically providing checks and balances, in practice creates opportunities for miscommunication and poor coordination.

Government auditors documented a particularly egregious example of these coordination failures: the Army purchased a $2.8 million piece of equipment in 2020 that cannot perform the job it was purchased to do. The failure resulted from poor coordination between headquarters officials responsible for equipment selection and plant-level officials who understood operational requirements. Formal governing documents do not define a role for plant officials beyond the initial selection stage for modernization projects, meaning that headquarters officials lacked a defined process for including plant expertise in later decision-making stages. The equipment, once delivered, proved incompatible with plant requirements, a waste of nearly three million dollars at a time when every resource directed toward ammunition production capacity represents strategic investment.

This incident illustrates a broader pattern: modernization decisions made without adequate input from those who will operate the facilities result in misaligned investments that fail to achieve intended capability improvements. The problem is compounded by the absence of systematic lessons-learned processes. When coordination failures occur at one plant, there is no mechanism to ensure that other facilities avoid similar mistakes. Each plant operates with different contracting approaches, different vendor relationships, and different coordination mechanisms, yet there is no systematic collection, analysis, validation, or sharing of lessons learned across the ammunition enterprise.

The financial implications of these coordination failures extend beyond individual equipment purchases. Modernization projects delayed by organizational confusion postpone capability improvements that could increase production rates or reduce costs. When plant officials and headquarters organizations disagree about whether a project constitutes maintenance (vendor responsibility) or modernization (government responsibility), the resulting delays mean that facilities operate with degraded equipment while disputes are resolved through bureaucratic channels. The time required to navigate these organizational ambiguities directly translates into reduced surge capacity and increased vulnerability during periods when adversaries can scale production more rapidly.

The management of contracts at government-owned, contractor-operated ammunition plants reveals additional layers of dysfunction that constrain the ability to rapidly scale production or adapt to changing requirements. Each of the five plants operates under different contracting approaches, different contract types, different performance periods, different maintenance definitions, different pricing structures, reflecting attempts to address unique challenges at individual facilities. While customization can be appropriate, the absence of systematic knowledge-sharing means that each plant reinvents solutions to common problems without benefiting from lessons learned elsewhere.

The variation in contracting approaches stems partly from attempts to address a fundamental challenge: how to incentivize private vendors to invest in government-owned facilities when contract periods may be too short to recover investment costs. The Army has experimented with contract periods ranging from ten to twenty-five years, included requirements for annual capital improvements, and structured various cost-sharing arrangements. Yet vendor officials at four of five plants reported that they still lack sufficient incentive to make significant investments in facility improvements. The economic logic is straightforward: capital investments require multi-year payback periods, but contract uncertainties and the possibility of not winning recompetition create risks that rational firms are reluctant to accept.

This investment hesitancy has direct consequences for surge capacity. Facilities operating with aging equipment, outdated processes, and inadequate infrastructure cannot rapidly scale production when demand increases. Modernization funded by government appropriations proceeds through bureaucratic channels that add years to timelines, while vendor-funded improvements remain limited due to uncertain return-on-investment calculations. The result is an industrial base that operates below potential efficiency during peacetime and lacks the flexibility to surge during crises, precisely the opposite of what strategic requirements demand.

The contracting approaches also reveal confusion about the allocation of costs between maintenance and modernization, creating ongoing disputes that consume organizational attention and delay necessary work. Performance work statements at the five plants include different definitions for various types of maintenance, attempting to clarify which repairs are vendor responsibility (funded through product sales) and which are government responsibility (funded through appropriations). Yet officials at multiple plants reported difficulties determining responsibility for specific projects, particularly for substantial repairs that exceed defined cost thresholds or involve ambiguous categories like replacing aging infrastructure with modern equivalents.

These definitional disputes have strategic consequences during efforts to scale production. When increased output requires facility modifications, organizational uncertainty about funding responsibility can delay implementation while bureaucratic processes determine whether the work constitutes maintenance or modernization. Environmental permits, safety reviews, and regulatory approvals add additional months or years to timelines. The cumulative effect is that even when funding is available and technical solutions are known, bureaucratic processes impose temporal constraints that can exceed the duration of the military operations the ammunition is meant to support.

The financial structures governing ammunition production reveal additional complexities that affect the government's ability to obtain cost-effective supplies while maintaining viable commercial operations at the plants. The Army typically structures contracts so that vendors perform facility maintenance and operations at no direct cost to the government, with these costs instead included in the prices of ammunition sold under supply contracts. This approach theoretically provides efficiency by consolidating costs, but it creates challenges in establishing fair pricing and ensuring equitable allocation of facility costs between government and commercial sales.

Several plants produce ammunition for both government and commercial customers, using government-owned equipment and facilities. The allocation of facility operation costs between these customer categories has proven contentious, with different plants adopting different approaches and vendors arguing that government-imposed requirements, extensive security forces, acceptance of deliveries at unusual hours, compliance with regulations beyond commercial norms, create costs that make government-funded production uncompetitive in commercial markets if fully loaded into product prices.

The Army has experimented with various pricing models, including price matrices that establish predictable costs for different quantity ranges, direct payment of facility costs separate from product prices, and profit-sharing arrangements where commercial sales revenue supports facility operations. Each approach has advantages and disadvantages, and government auditors documented instances where pricing structures produced unintended consequences. At one plant, the Army transitioned from including facility costs in product prices to paying these costs directly, but this change resulted in the government paying an additional $15.7 million in 2019 because costs to operate the facility were not allocated to all customers. The Army subsequently modified the contract to return to the previous approach, but only after absorbing substantial additional costs.

complications directly affect the government's ability to obtain ammunition at reasonable costs while maintaining the industrial base necessary for surge production. If facility operation costs are fully loaded into government ammunition prices to ensure commercial competitiveness, the government pays more than a strict cost-accounting would suggest is appropriate. If facility costs are shared across all production, commercial ammunition may be priced above market rates, reducing commercial sales that help maintain workforce skills and equipment utilization. Either approach creates inefficiencies, but the absence of systematic analysis comparing approaches across plants means the Army lacks empirical basis for determining optimal pricing structures.

Case Study: Modern Small-Arms Economics

The U.S. Army's Next Generation Squad Weapon (NGSW) program illustrates how technological advances can exacerbate industrial constraints. While the 6.8 mm ammunition family offers greater lethality, each round costs in the double digit dollar range unsustainable in any high-intensity conflict where daily consumption reaches hundreds of thousands. The Oshkosh Joint Light Tactical

Vehicle, similarly, embodies technological progress but limited production throughput: modernization contracts worth tens of millions translate to only modest delivery rates. Such examples underscore your broader argument that capability gains are being purchased at the expense of logistical and industrial coherence.

A critical issue identified in government audits is the absence of systematic processes for collecting, analyzing, validating, archiving, and sharing lessons learned related to ammunition procurement and production. Despite managing five government owned, contractor operated (GOCO) plants with different vendors and contracting approaches, the Army has not established mechanisms to ensure that insights from one facility inform decisions at others. When officials at one plant develop innovative solutions to coordination challenges or contracting problems, this knowledge remains localized rather than being systematically shared throughout the ammunition enterprise.

The implications of this organizational amnesia are profound. The Army awarded contracts for two plants in 2019 but did not formally share lessons learned between the acquisition teams, meaning that each team independently addressed challenges that the other had already confronted. Government auditors noted that the Army was competing another contract during the audit period but had not established processes to share lessons learned from previous competitions with the current acquisition team. This pattern ensures that the organization repeatedly encounters similar problems without building institutional knowledge about effective solutions.

Government auditors identified leading practices for lessons-learned processes: collecting information through systematic methods, analyzing information to determine root causes, validating applicability of lessons across different contexts, storing and archiving lessons in accessible repositories, and disseminating lessons through multiple channels. Army officials acknowledged that implementing such processes would be beneficial, and some limited efforts exist, integrated product team meetings occasionally discuss lessons informally, and a 2021 GAO study recommended capturing lessons learned, but no comprehensive system has been established or sustained.

The absence of lessons-learned processes means that each organizational transition, each contract competition, and each modernization effort starts from limited institutional memory rather than building on accumulated experience. When personnel change, knowledge walks out the door. When new challenges arise, solutions must be developed anew rather than adapting approaches that proved effective elsewhere. This organizational inefficiency compounds the industrial capacity constraints documented in previous chapters, ensuring that even modest attempts to improve performance encounter unnecessary obstacles.

The organizational pathologies documented in government audits create strategic vulnerabilities that extend beyond the mathematical constraints of production capacity. Even if funding were unlimited, skilled workers abundant, and supply chains resilient, the bureaucratic structures managing ammunition production would constrain the ability to rapidly respond to wartime demands. Unclear lines of authority delay decisions. Outdated governing documents create confusion about responsibilities. Coordination failures result in wasted investments. Contracting complexities slow facility improvements. Pricing disputes consume organizational attention. The absence of lessons-learned processes ensures that mistakes are repeated rather than corrected.

These dysfunctions are particularly consequential because they are largely invisible to external observers and resistant to rapid reform. Increasing appropriations does not clarify organizational responsibilities. Hiring additional staff does not resolve coordination failures between offices with intersecting authorities. Demanding faster production does not eliminate bureaucratic review processes embedded in regulations and procedures. The temporal dimension of these constraints means that organizational reform requires sustained effort over years or decades, timescales that far exceed the duration of military conflicts these systems are meant to support.

The contrast with adversary approaches is instructive. China's Military-Civil Fusion strategy eliminates many of the organizational boundaries that create coordination challenges in Western systems. Russian ammunition production, while facing its own constraints, operates within clearer hierarchies and with fewer regulatory obstacles to rapid scaling. North Korea's willingness to provide millions of shells to Russia demonstrates the advantage of centralized decision-making unconstrained by the bureaucratic processes that Western democracies consider essential for accountability and transparency.

The fundamental tension is that the organizational structures creating these dysfunctions serve legitimate purposes during peacetime: ensuring accountability, preventing waste, maintaining safety, protecting the environment, and preserving competition. The regulations requiring environmental reviews, the contracting procedures mandating competition, the oversight mechanisms demanding documentation, all reflect democratic values and lessons learned from past abuses. Yet these same structures become liabilities when rapid scaling is required, creating a dilemma that democratic societies have not successfully resolved: how to maintain peacetime accountability while preserving wartime agility.

The government auditors' recommendations, revise governing documents, establish lessons-learned processes, clarify roles and responsibilities, are sensible and necessary. Yet the fact that similar recommendations have been made repeatedly over decades, with limited implementation, suggests that organizational reform faces obstacles beyond simple neglect or insufficient priority. The distributed authority that creates coordination challenges also serves as a check on concentrated power. The multiple organizations with intersecting responsibilities provide redundancy that can catch errors. The complex contracting procedures reflect accumulated lessons about preventing fraud and ensuring fair competition. Simplifying these structures would create efficiencies but also risks that democratic institutions are designed to mitigate.

The strategic implication is that Western military establishments must plan for sustained conflicts while acknowledging that their industrial bases operate under organizational constraints that adversaries do not face. The production rates, scaling timelines, and surge capabilities that are theoretically possible may remain practically unachievable due to bureaucratic structures that cannot be rapidly reformed without compromising the accountability and transparency that democratic governance demands. This recognition should inform force planning, operational concepts, and strategic commitments: the industrial base supporting military operations is not only constrained by mathematics of production but also by organizational pathologies that compound temporal asymmetries and limit strategic flexibility.

The Ukraine conflict has exposed these vulnerabilities with unprecedented clarity, demonstrating that Western ammunition production cannot rapidly scale to meet sustained high-intensity operations. The government's own auditors have documented that organizational dysfunction compounds these constraints, creating bureaucratic bottlenecks that would persist even if financial resources and technical capabilities were unlimited. The challenge for democratic societies is not merely to increase production capacity but to reform organizational structures in ways that preserve accountability while enabling responsiveness, a tension that has no obvious resolution and that adversaries may exploit with increasing sophistication in the strategic competition that defines the twenty-first century.

Chapter 10

The Dependency Paradox: Adversary Components in American Arsenals

The preceding chapters have established that Western defense industrial capacity cannot sustain the consumption rates observed in prolonged high-intensity conflicts, that regulatory and workforce constraints prevent rapid scaling, and that supply chain dependencies create strategic vulnerabilities. Yet these analyses, while documenting severe limitations, operate under an assumption that has become increasingly untenable: that the United States and its allies possess sufficient visibility into their defense supply chains to assess, let alone mitigate, these dependencies. A comprehensive examination of recent government oversight findings reveals that this assumption is false. The Department of Defense lacks fundamental knowledge about where critical components of its most advanced weapon systems originate, cannot compel contractors to provide this information, and has discovered adversary-sourced materials in operational military hardware only through contractor self-disclosure and fortuitous inspections rather than systematic oversight.

This revelation transforms the strategic calculus documented in earlier chapters. The question is no longer merely whether Western industrial capacity can surge rapidly enough to meet wartime demands, but whether current production depends on continued access to suppliers controlled by potential adversaries. If the answer is affirmative, and mounting evidence suggests it is, then the temporal asymmetries, production bottlenecks, and mobilization constraints identified throughout this analysis become secondary to a more fundamental problem: the United States cannot independently produce the weapons systems it would deploy in conflicts with the very nations supplying components for those systems.

The Visibility Gap

In July 2025, the Government Accountability Office published findings that fundamentally challenge assumptions about defense supply chain security. The report, mandated by Congress to assess the degree to which the Department of Defense depends on foreign entities for procurement of goods essential to national security, documented systematic failures in tracking the origins of components throughout the defense industrial base. The scale of the problem is staggering: the Department of Defense relies on a network exceeding 200,000 suppliers to produce advanced weapon systems and noncombat goods, yet the primary federal procurement database provides minimal insight into where these goods are manufactured or whether materials and component suppliers are domestic or foreign.

The Federal Procurement Data System, which serves as the government-wide repository for contract information, records two data fields ostensibly related to foreign sourcing: Place of Manufacture and Country of Product or Service Origin. Analysis of these fields for fiscal years 2020 through 2024 reveals that the United States is identified as the country of origin for approximately 96 percent of defense procurement obligations by dollar value. This statistic, frequently cited in assessments of industrial base resilience, obscures rather than illuminates the actual structure of defense supply chains. The database records the location of final assembly or the country from which the preponderance of content derives, not the origins of sub-tier components, raw materials, or critical subsystems that determine whether production can continue independently of foreign suppliers.

Department of Defense officials acknowledged to government auditors that the Federal Procurement Data System cannot determine where components of procured goods are produced. This admission is not trivial administrative detail but rather a confession of strategic blindness. When the department cannot identify component origins, it cannot assess supply chain vulnerabilities, cannot anticipate disruptions, and cannot develop mitigation strategies until crises materialize. The statistical mirage of domestic sourcing, 96 percent appearing as United States origin despite pervasive foreign dependencies, creates false confidence in industrial self-sufficiency that evaporates when examined against actual supply chain structures.

The consequences of this visibility gap extend throughout the defense industrial base. Government auditors examined the F-35 Joint Strike Fighter, the most expensive weapons program in American history, and found that the Federal Procurement Data System identified the United States as the country of origin for 114 of 115 active contracts related to the aircraft between fiscal years 2020 and 2024. Yet the database contains no information on the subcontracts that the prime contractor, Lockheed Martin, maintains with suppliers providing subsystems, components, and raw materials. Department of Defense officials conceded that determining the actual origin of F-35 components requires information not captured in government procurement systems, information that exists, if at all, in contractor databases that the government cannot access without contractual authority it has not established.

The inadequacy of existing oversight mechanisms became undeniable when Lockheed Martin disclosed to the Department of Defense in 2023 and 2024 that magnets manufactured in China had been integrated into F-35 aircraft. These magnets, composed of materials prohibited by statute from adversarial sources, were discovered not through Department of Defense supply chain monitoring but through contractor internal reviews. The disclosure triggered production stoppages lasting approximately six months in both instances while the department assessed risks, validated alternative suppliers, and issued national security waivers to accept aircraft containing the prohibited materials.

The statutory prohibition on Chinese magnets reflects congressional recognition that certain materials pose unacceptable supply chain risks. Section 871 of the John S. McCain National Defense Authorization Act for Fiscal Year 2019 specifically prohibits acquisition of samarium-cobalt magnets, neodymium-iron-boron magnets, tungsten metal powder, and tungsten heavy alloys from China, Iran, North Korea, or Russia unless specific exceptions apply. The integration of Chinese magnets into F-35s despite this explicit prohibition demonstrates that statutory restrictions alone cannot ensure compliance when visibility into sub-tier suppliers remains limited and contractors face no systematic requirements to verify component origins.

The department's response to the magnet disclosures illuminates both the limitations of current oversight and the strategic calculations that govern procurement decisions. Officials issued national security waivers accepting the aircraft with Chinese magnets, determining that the magnets posed no safety risk and that national security interests justified proceeding with deliveries rather than sustaining prolonged production disruptions. This decision, while pragmatic given immediate operational requirements, establishes precedent that strategic imperatives can override statutory prohibitions when supply chain dependencies become apparent only after integration into operational systems. The waiver mechanism, intended for exceptional circumstances, risks becoming routine accommodation of dependencies that systematic oversight would have prevented.

Government auditors documented that the Department of Defense subsequently used a supply chain risk evaluation tool to identify alternative suppliers for the magnets, demonstrating reactive rather than proactive risk management. The tool, known as Supply Chain Risk Evaluation Environment or SCREEn, was initiated in 2020 to gain visibility into F-35 microelectronics and propulsion supply chains. As of April 2025, SCREEn contained country-of-origin data for first- and second-tier suppliers for 30,000 of approximately 40,000 F-35 parts, representing significant progress but leaving substantial gaps. Officials estimated that they have collected country-of-origin information on less than 10 percent of all suppliers providing components and raw materials for those parts, meaning that visibility extends to major subsystems but not to the granular level where materials like specialized magnets enter the supply chain.

The magnet incident was not isolated. During a site visit to the prime contractor, Department of Defense program officials identified Chinese-made robotic arms in the F-35 assembly line, manufactured by a German company subsequently acquired by Chinese interests. This discovery triggered an investigation revealing cybersecurity concerns, which the department mitigated by instructing the contractor to disconnect the robots from internet connectivity. The officials concluded that the robotic arms posed no safety or quality impacts to the aircraft, but the episode underscores how foreign ownership and control can manifest at unexpected points in production processes. Manufacturing equipment, while not incorporated into the final product, provides potential access to proprietary designs, production specifications, and assembly processes that constitute strategic intellectual property.

These revelations about the F-35 program carry implications that extend far beyond a single weapons system. The aircraft represents the pinnacle of American aerospace engineering, incorporates the most advanced technologies available, and operates under acquisition oversight more intensive than virtually any other defense program. If supply chain visibility for the F-35 remains incomplete despite these extraordinary circumstances, the situation for less scrutinized programs and lower-priority systems is necessarily worse. The patterns documented in F-35 supply chain analysis, reliance on contractor self-disclosure, reactive rather than proactive risk identification, acceptance of foreign dependencies discovered after integration, likely characterize defense procurement across the enterprise.

The strategic vulnerabilities revealed through the F-35 magnet and robotic arm incidents pale in comparison to the pervasive dependencies that characterize microelectronics supply chains. Department of Defense estimates indicate that 88 percent of microelectronics production and 98 percent of assembly, packaging, and testing occur overseas, with manufacturing concentrated primarily in Taiwan, South Korea, and China. These components pervade virtually every defense system: precision-guided munitions depend on microprocessors for targeting calculations, communication systems require integrated circuits for signal processing, sensors rely on semiconductors for data collection, and command and control networks function through computational infrastructure built on globally sourced electronics.

The geographic concentration of microelectronics manufacturing creates dependencies that cannot be rapidly mitigated. Taiwan Semiconductor Manufacturing Company alone produces over half of the world's semiconductors and controls even higher percentages of the most advanced chips used in military systems. Modern semiconductor fabrication facilities, known as fabs, require investments measured in tens of billions of dollars and construction timescales extending multiple years before production begins. The specialized equipment used in these facilities, lithography systems, deposition chambers, etching tools, is itself produced by a limited number of suppliers, creating additional bottlenecks that constrain any efforts to establish alternative production sources.

Government auditors examined Department of Defense procurement of electronic microcircuits, a category of microelectronics, and found that the Federal Procurement Data System identified the United States as both Place of Manufacture and Country of Origin for nearly 100 percent of $1.3 billion in obligations between fiscal years 2020 and 2024. Defense Microelectronics Activity officials explained that over $400 million of these procurements involved microcircuits from accredited trusted suppliers using commercial domestic foundry processes, addressing defense-unique requirements that commercially available components could not satisfy. However, Department of Defense officials expressed concern that commercial microelectronics incorporated into defense goods originate overwhelmingly from non-United States sources despite appearing as domestic in procurement databases.

This definitional discrepancy, whereby components are recorded as domestic based on where they are packaged or tested rather than where underlying semiconductors are manufactured, obscures the true structure of microelectronics dependencies. A chip designed in the United States, fabricated in Taiwan using specialized equipment from the Netherlands, assembled in Malaysia, and tested in the United States before integration into a weapon system may be recorded as domestic origin if the final testing occurs domestically. This statistical artifact creates the appearance of supply chain security while masking dependencies that would become critical constraints during conflicts that disrupt access to overseas manufacturing capacity.

The strategic implications become particularly acute when considering Taiwan's dual role as both the dominant microelectronics manufacturer and a potential theater of conflict. Scenarios involving military operations in the Taiwan Strait would simultaneously create peak demand for precision munitions requiring advanced semiconductors while potentially disrupting access to the facilities producing those semiconductors. This creates a paradox whereby the very weapons systems required to conduct operations would depend on continued access to manufacturing capacity in the conflict zone itself. Planning assumptions that treat microelectronics supply as assured during wartime operations ignore this fundamental tension between operational requirements and industrial dependencies.

The vulnerability is not limited to advanced microelectronics and sophisticated weapon systems. Government auditors documented that even artillery ammunition, seemingly straightforward munitions whose designs have remained relatively stable for decades, involves supply chains with foreign dependencies that Department of Defense visibility efforts have only partially mapped. The Army developed an Industrial Base Analysis Tool to model the ammunition industrial base using government and commercial data, leveraging advantages that arise because the Department of Defense develops ammunition designs and owns associated data rights. This tool enabled the Army to achieve significantly more supply chain visibility for ammunition than for other categories of defense materiel.

Analysis using this tool identified several Chinese sources in the 155 millimeter ammunition supply chain. Government auditors did not specify whether these sources provide raw materials, components, or manufacturing equipment, nor did they indicate the scale of dependency or whether alternative suppliers exist. The identification of Chinese involvement in ammunition supply chains is concerning precisely because ammunition represents the category of defense materiel most urgently needed in sustained conflicts and most difficult to substitute through alternatives when supply chains are disrupted. Unlike complex systems that might be preserved through careful operational employment, artillery shells are consumed in quantities that exhaust stockpiles within weeks or months of intensive operations.

The Ukraine conflict has demonstrated that artillery ammunition consumption during high-intensity operations far exceeds peacetime production capacity, forcing difficult choices between supporting allies and maintaining domestic stockpiles. If the production capacity that Western nations are struggling to scale depends on continued access to suppliers in potential adversary nations, then the mathematical constraints on surge production documented in earlier chapters become compounded by political vulnerabilities. Adversaries aware of these dependencies could leverage supply restrictions as tools of coercion, threatening to constrain Western ammunition production at precisely the moments when sustained operations require maximum output.

The extent of dependency remains unclear because systematic mapping of ammunition supply chains is incomplete. The Army's Industrial Base Analysis Tool represents progress toward visibility, but government auditors noted that even with this tool, comprehensive understanding of sub-tier suppliers and raw materials sources remains elusive. Specialized chemicals for propellants, high-grade steel for shell casings, electronic components for fuzes, and rare earth elements for various applications all flow through global supply networks that may include Chinese sources at multiple tiers. Without complete visibility, the Department of Defense cannot assess whether scaling ammunition production would strain dependent supply chains or whether alternative sources could be activated within operationally relevant timescales.

The persistent gaps in supply chain visibility reflect not merely inadequate data collection but rather fundamental structural limitations in how the Department of Defense procures goods and services. Prime contractors are not contractually required to provide country-of-origin information for sub-tier suppliers, and voluntary efforts to collect this information have achieved limited success. Government auditors documented the Defense Logistics Agency's attempt to map supply chains across three classes of goods, aviation parts, clothing and textiles, and land and maritime parts, by surveying 63 suppliers. Of these suppliers, 37 agreed to provide information, 22 declined to participate or were non-responsive, and four were still evaluating whether they would participate as of the audit period.

Suppliers declining to participate cited several concerns: absence of contractual obligations to provide the information, additional workload requirements, limited resources to dedicate to data collection efforts, and unwillingness to share proprietary information that might benefit competitors or reveal business relationships they consider confidential. Defense Logistics Agency officials concluded that limited supplier participation negated any analytical value from the effort and stated that obtaining additional supplier information would require contract clauses establishing mandatory disclosure requirements. This finding underscores that voluntary cooperation, while preferable from contractor perspectives, proves insufficient when systematic visibility is needed across the entire defense industrial base.

The Department of Defense faces competing considerations in deciding whether to mandate supply chain disclosure through contract requirements. Some officials assert that supplier information already exists in enterprise resource planning systems that contractors maintain for inventory management and production planning, suggesting that providing this information to the government would impose minimal additional costs. These officials note that private sector companies have successfully gained supply chain visibility by requiring sub-tier suppliers to share information from existing databases, implying that similar approaches could work for defense procurement.

However, other officials and industry representatives contend that mandatory disclosure requirements would significantly increase costs, particularly if imposed after contracts are awarded and production has commenced. They suggest that the Department of Defense should limit disclosure requirements to critical components and technologies or to new acquisition programs early in development, where supply chain considerations can be integrated into initial contract structures. Industry representatives also express concern about inadequate safeguards to protect proprietary information from disclosure to competitors, arguing that supply chain data reveals business relationships and sourcing strategies that constitute competitive advantages in commercial markets.

Additional complications arise from supplier concerns about liability and penalties when foreign dependencies surface. The F-35 production stoppages following magnet disclosures, during which Department of Defense payments to the contractor ceased for approximately six months, demonstrate that revealing supply chain issues can impose significant financial consequences. Suppliers aware of such precedents face disincentives to disclose potential foreign dependency risks, particularly when the regulatory and contractual framework for how the department will respond remains unclear. Department of Defense officials acknowledged that addressing these concerns would likely require determinations about the extent to which suppliers could receive protection from liability or penalties when foreign dependencies are identified through disclosure rather than concealment.

The department has not yet tested whether contractual requirements for supply chain disclosure would effectively provide needed visibility or what costs and challenges such requirements would entail. Government auditors noted that the Department of Defense remains in conceptual phases of developing potential contract clauses rather than piloting approaches to assess feasibility. Good practices for enterprise risk management indicate that agencies should consider costs and benefits of proposed risk mitigation approaches before full implementation. Testing disclosure requirements through pilot programs on selected contracts would provide empirical data on implementation challenges, costs, supplier resistance, and the quality of information obtained, insights essential for determining whether and how to scale such requirements across the defense industrial base.

Beyond data collection challenges, the Department of Defense confronts organizational fragmentation that inhibits effective use of whatever supply chain information exists. Multiple organizations across the department, the Office of Industrial Base Policy, the Deputy Assistant Secretary for Logistics, the Chief Digital and Artificial

Intelligence Office, individual military services, and various program offices, have initiated efforts to enhance supply chain visibility, but these efforts remain uncoordinated and provide little integration of findings across organizational boundaries. Government auditors identified this fragmentation as impeding the development of a holistic framework for managing supply chain risks, including risks of foreign dependency.

The department established a Supply Chain Risk Management Integration Center in November 2024 to address coordination deficiencies, but as of the government audit completion in July 2025, officials had not identified resources, priorities, and time frames for the office to implement integration activities. Officials explained that they needed to ensure that planned actions align with the current Secretary of Defense's priorities before committing to specific implementation approaches. This hesitation to move forward, while reflecting appropriate deference to political leadership, means that organizational fragmentation persists despite recognition that it constrains effective risk management.

The absence of systematic integration mechanisms means that insights gained in one program or organization may not inform decisions elsewhere. When the F-35 program identified Chinese magnets and robotic arms, this knowledge did not automatically trigger reviews of other aircraft programs using similar components or manufacturing processes. When the Army's Industrial Base Analysis Tool identified Chinese sources in ammunition supply chains, this finding did not necessarily prompt comparable analyses for other kinetic capabilities or different types of munitions. Each organization and program confronts supply chain vulnerabilities independently, reinventing analytical approaches and potentially discovering the same dependencies multiple times through disconnected processes.

Government auditors in January 2025 examined commercial sector leading practices for supply chain visibility and compared them to Department of Defense approaches. The auditors identified six areas where department practices diverged from leading practices and recommended twelve specific improvements. Key recommendations included establishing priorities for visibility efforts rather than attempting comprehensive mapping immediately, mandating contract clauses requiring data sharing from suppliers, focusing initial efforts on high-risk supply chain items and new contracts where requirements can be incorporated efficiently, and developing systematic processes for collecting, analyzing, and sharing supply chain risk information across organizational boundaries.

Department of Defense officials concurred with the recommendations but have not yet designated the organizations responsible for implementing them or established timelines for completion. This pattern, acknowledging problems, accepting recommendations, but delaying implementation pending alignment with leadership priorities, suggests that supply chain visibility improvements will proceed incrementally rather than through systematic transformation. The temporal dimension matters critically because the longer these organizational and contractual limitations persist, the more deeply embedded foreign dependencies become in existing systems and the more difficult they are to identify and mitigate when geopolitical circumstances change.

The implications of pervasive supply chain dependencies and limited visibility extend throughout the strategic calculations that guide defense planning. Earlier chapters documented that Western ammunition production cannot sustain consumption rates observed in prolonged conflicts, that regulatory and workforce constraints prevent rapid scaling, and that adversaries with different industrial models can outproduce democratic societies in attritional competitions. These findings assumed, however, that Western production capacity, though limited, operates independently of adversary control. The discoveries documented in government oversight reports challenge this assumption, revealing that current production depends on continued access to suppliers that potential adversaries may control or influence.

This dependency creates vulnerabilities that adversaries can exploit through multiple mechanisms. Direct supply restrictions represent the most obvious risk: nations controlling critical materials or components can threaten to curtail supplies during crises, forcing target nations to choose between operational requirements and acquiescence to political demands. The concentration of rare earth processing in China provides paradigmatic example: if Chinese authorities restricted exports of materials essential for precision munitions, Western nations would face immediate constraints on production capacity for weapons required to deter or respond to Chinese military operations. The temporal asymmetry between the speed at which supply restrictions take effect and the years required to establish alternative sources amplifies coercive leverage.

Subtler vulnerabilities arise from dependencies on components whose reliability or security could be compromised. Microelectronics manufactured in facilities subject to foreign intelligence services' influence might incorporate backdoors or vulnerabilities that could be exploited during conflicts. Manufacturing equipment produced by companies under foreign government control could provide access to proprietary designs and production specifications. Even seemingly benign components like magnets or structural materials, if sourced from adversary nations, create points in supply chains where quality, availability, or specifications could be manipulated to degrade system performance without detection until operational failures materialize.

The visibility limitations documented in government audits mean that the Department of Defense cannot comprehensively assess the scope of these vulnerabilities. Knowing that Chinese magnets appeared in F-35s and that Chinese sources exist in ammunition supply chains provides data points, but systematic understanding requires mapping dependencies across the full range of weapons systems, munitions, and supporting equipment. Without such mapping, the department cannot prioritize mitigation efforts, cannot assess whether alternative suppliers exist at reasonable costs, and cannot determine whether current acquisition strategies inadvertently increase rather than decrease dependencies over time.

The strategic calculus becomes particularly complex when considering that many foreign dependencies arise not from deliberate decisions to source from adversaries but from the structure of global industrial networks that evolved during periods of reduced geopolitical tensions. Semiconductor manufacturing concentrated in East Asia because firms there achieved technological leadership and cost advantages, not because Western governments strategically chose to depend on Asian suppliers. Rare earth processing shifted to China because Chinese companies accepted environmental costs and made industrial investments that Western firms declined, not because of conscious decisions to cede control of critical materials. These dependencies emerged through market forces and accumulated incrementally until they became deeply embedded in industrial structures that cannot be rapidly restructured.

Addressing these dependencies requires not merely procurement reforms but fundamental changes in industrial organization, regulatory frameworks, and investment priorities that extend far beyond Department of Defense authorities. Establishing domestic microelectronics manufacturing capacity sufficient to meet defense requirements necessitates subsidies measured in hundreds of billions of dollars, regulatory accommodations to expedite facility construction, and coordinated efforts to develop workforce skills that have eroded through decades of offshoring. Similar challenges characterize efforts to rebuild domestic capacity for rare earth processing, specialized chemicals, advanced materials, and other categories where foreign dependencies have become entrenched.

The temporal dimension compounds these difficulties because supply chain restructuring requires years to implement while geopolitical conditions can shift rapidly. Investments initiated today to reduce dependencies on Chinese suppliers will not mature until the late 2020s at earliest, assuming political will sustains efforts across administration changes and competing budget priorities. During this transition period, dependencies persist and may actually increase as existing systems age and require components from established supply chains. The risk emerges that dependencies become most acute precisely when geopolitical tensions reach levels where adversaries might consider exploiting supply chain leverage.

The Taiwan Paradox

The concentration of microelectronics manufacturing in Taiwan creates perhaps the most acute expression of supply chain vulnerability because it combines extreme dependency with high probability that a conflict scenario would disrupt access. Taiwan Semiconductor Manufacturing Company's dominance in advanced chip production means that virtually every sophisticated American weapon system depends on continued access to Taiwanese manufacturing capacity. Simultaneously, Taiwan remains among the most likely potential conflict zones given persistent tensions with China and the strategic importance both sides attach to the island's status.

This creates paradoxical dependencies whereby the weapons systems required to defend Taiwan or deter Chinese military operations depend on manufacturing capacity located on the island itself. A conflict that disrupted Taiwanese semiconductor production would simultaneously create peak demand for precision munitions requiring advanced chips while eliminating access to the facilities producing those chips. Planning for sustained operations in such scenarios requires either enormous stockpiles assembled before conflicts begin, stockpiles whose size would be constrained by the very production limitations this scenario contemplates, or alternative sources of microelectronics that currently do not exist at scale.

The Taiwanese case illustrates broader principles about how geographic concentration of critical manufacturing capacity creates strategic vulnerabilities that extend beyond immediate supply disruptions. Even if alternative semiconductor facilities existed in allied nations, conflicts affecting Taiwan would likely disrupt global electronics supply chains sufficiently to constrain access to components for numerous industries simultaneously. The resulting competition for limited supplies would force prioritization decisions about which systems receive available chips, potentially leaving lower-priority but operationally necessary systems without sustainment. The complexity of modern weapon systems means that shortage of any single critical component can render entire platforms inoperable regardless of the availability of other parts.

The Department of Defense has pursued several initiatives intended to mitigate foreign dependency risks once identified, including investments through Defense Production Act Title III authorities, policy changes prohibiting procurement of specific items from designated countries, maintenance of strategic stockpiles for critical materials, and partnerships with allied nations to expand production capacity outside adversary control. These initiatives represent appropriate responses but remain inadequate to address dependencies whose scope remains incompletely understood and whose resolution requires industrial transformations extending beyond department authorities or budgets.

Investment programs provide tools for addressing specific identified gaps but cannot systematically reduce dependencies across the entire industrial base. The Department obligated approximately $6.5 billion through three primary investment programs for 828 projects between fiscal years 2020 and 2024, supporting efforts to restore domestic production of critical chemicals, expand solid rocket motor manufacturing, and develop advanced manufacturing technologies. These investments, while substantial, address targeted vulnerabilities rather than comprehensively restructuring supply chains. Absent complete visibility into dependencies, investment decisions risk focusing on known problems while unknown vulnerabilities persist.

Policy prohibitions on procurement from adversary nations face implementation challenges when supply chain visibility remains limited. Statutory restrictions on Chinese magnets did not prevent their integration into F-35s because the restrictions could not be enforced without the visibility necessary to track component origins through multiple supply tiers. Expanding prohibitions to additional categories of goods or materials would face similar enforcement challenges unless accompanied by contractual requirements compelling suppliers to disclose origins, requirements that, as documented earlier, the Department has not yet tested or implemented systematically.

Strategic stockpiles provide buffers against supply disruptions but cannot substitute for independent production capacity during sustained operations. The National Defense Stockpile maintained by the Department of Defense holds approximately 50 types of materials, primarily raw materials and basic elements rather than manufactured components or subassemblies. Government auditors previously reported that the Department depends on foreign or single domestic sources for over half of the 99 materials identified as potential shortfalls, including materials not currently held in stockpiles. While Congress appropriated $175 million in fiscal years 2022 and 2024 to acquire additional materials, stockpiles sufficient to sustain multi-year high-intensity operations would require resources far exceeding these initial investments and would need regular rotation to prevent degradation.

Partnerships with allied nations expand the geographic distribution of production capacity but do not eliminate dependencies when allies themselves rely on adversary sources for raw materials or components. The Army's partnership with Canadian firms to increase ammunition production, cited as example of successful international collaboration, may reduce concentration risk but does not address underlying questions about whether Canadian facilities depend on Chinese suppliers for specialized chemicals, rare earth elements, or other inputs. Similarly, Defense Production Act investments in Canadian companies to strengthen cobalt and graphite supply chains may diversify sourcing but require verification that the beneficiary companies do not themselves depend on Chinese precursor materials or processing capacity.

The Unanswered Questions

The July 2025 Government Accountability Office report raised fundamental questions about Department of Defense supply chain visibility and dependency risks, but many of the most strategically significant questions remain unanswered. The Department does not know the full extent of adversary presence in defense supply chains, cannot reliably predict which systems would be most affected by supply disruptions, and has not determined whether current production could continue if access to specific foreign suppliers were severed. These information gaps persist despite recognition that they constitute strategic vulnerabilities and despite congressional direction to improve visibility and mitigate dependencies.

The case of 155 millimeter ammunition illustrates the practical consequences of incomplete visibility. Government auditors documented that the Army identified several Chinese sources in ammunition supply chains but provided no details about whether these sources supply raw materials, intermediate products, or specialized components; whether alternative suppliers exist at comparable costs and capacities; or whether planned production increases to support Ukraine and replenish stocks depend on continued access to these sources. Without answers to these questions, assessments of ammunition production sustainability remain speculative, and planning for potential supply disruptions proceeds from incomplete information.

The F-35 revelations about Chinese magnets and robotic arms similarly raise questions whose answers remain unclear. Were these isolated instances or representative of broader patterns throughout the supply chain? Do other aircraft programs contain similar dependencies? Have the identified issues been resolved through alternative suppliers, or do they persist under national security waivers? What mechanisms ensure that future design changes or supplier transitions do not reintroduce dependencies? The reactive nature of risk identification, depending on contractor disclosures and fortuitous inspections rather than systematic monitoring, provides no assurance that currently unknown dependencies do not exist throughout operational systems.

The microelectronics dependencies represent perhaps the most consequential unanswered questions. The Department acknowledges that 88 percent of production and 98 percent of assembly occur overseas but has not publicly disclosed detailed assessments of how specific weapon systems would be affected by disruption of Taiwan Semiconductor Manufacturing Company operations, what alternative sources exist for the most advanced chips, how long establishing domestic production capacity sufficient to meet defense requirements would require, or whether current acquisition strategies are increasing or decreasing microelectronics dependencies over time. These questions admit no simple answers because global semiconductor supply chains involve complex interactions among design, fabrication, assembly, and testing activities distributed across multiple countries and dependent on specialized equipment and materials with their own concentrated supply chains.

The conventional narrative about Western military advantages assumes that technological sophistication, superior training, and advanced systems provide decisive edges over adversaries whose capabilities in these dimensions lag. This narrative, while capturing important aspects of military effectiveness, has understated the extent to which maintaining technological advantages depends on global supply chains that potential adversaries may influence or disrupt. The discovery of Chinese components in American weapons systems, the concentration of critical manufacturing in potentially contested regions, and the persistent gaps in supply chain visibility collectively suggest that technological superiority may be more fragile than traditional assessments acknowledge.

The implications extend beyond immediate supply chain risks to challenge assumptions about strategic competition and military planning. If sustaining current force structures depends on continued access to adversary suppliers, then deterrence becomes more complex because adversaries possess economic leverage that traditional military balances may not capture. If responding to conflicts requires weapons systems whose production depends on manufacturing capacity in the conflict zone itself, then operational planning must account for constraints that transcend tactical considerations about force employment. If Western nations cannot independently produce the munitions required for sustained operations, then alliance commitments become contingent on industrial capacity that political decisions and market forces have systematically eroded over decades.

The temporal dimension deserves particular emphasis because it transforms supply chain dependencies from technical procurement challenges into strategic vulnerabilities that may persist for decades. The Department of Defense can recognize problems, accept audit recommendations, and commit to improving visibility, but translating intentions into systematic changes requires confronting organizational inertia, regulatory constraints, workforce limitations, and capital requirements that constrain even well-resourced reform efforts. The same factors that prevent rapid scaling of ammunition production, specialized skills, regulatory processes, capital-intensive facilities, complex supply networks, also prevent rapid restructuring of dependencies once identified. Strategic competitors aware of these temporal constraints may calculate that Western recognition of vulnerabilities will not translate into meaningful reduction of dependencies within timeframes relevant to their planning horizons.

The uncomfortable reality emerging from these findings is that the United States and its allies have constructed military capabilities whose sustainability depends on industrial structures optimized for peacetime efficiency rather than wartime resilience. The same globalization that reduced costs and expanded access to cutting-edge technologies also created dependencies that strategic competitors might exploit during conflicts those technologies were intended to deter or win. Addressing these dependencies requires not merely technical adjustments to procurement processes but fundamental reconsiderations of how democratic societies balance efficiency against resilience, cost-effectiveness against independence, and access to advanced capabilities against the vulnerabilities that access creates. The mathematical constraints on ammunition production documented in earlier chapters, the regulatory obstacles to mobilization, and the temporal asymmetries favoring adversaries collectively reveal one dimension of strategic vulnerability. The supply chain dependencies examined in this chapter reveal another dimension, one that may prove even more difficult to address because it requires restructuring global industrial networks that decades of incremental decisions have rendered deeply resistant to rapid change.

Chapter 11

Policy Prescriptions Overcoming the Mobilization Impossibility and Production Paradox

The preceding chapters have traced the constraints on Western ammunition and defense production in detail, from mathematical limits to organizational dysfunction and strategic vulnerabilities. Understanding the problem is essential, but diagnosis alone cannot secure readiness. The "Mobilization Impossibility" and the "Production Paradox" demand deliberate, practical solutions, policies that reconcile democratic accountability with the ability to respond swiftly in crisis.

Legal and regulatory frameworks, while critical in peacetime, often become obstacles during emergencies. Western governments must create mechanisms that allow flexibility without sacrificing oversight. One approach is to designate "Defense Production Zones," regions where critical defense manufacturing can operate under pre-approved, crisis-specific rules. These Zones would not be activated arbitrarily; clear triggers should be legislated. For example, a Declaration of a Defense Production Emergency by the President or Prime Minister, a two-thirds vote in Congress or Parliament, or a formal request from NATO's supreme commander (SACEUR) could initiate "Surge Mode." Within such zones, permitting, environmental reviews, and logistical approvals could be expedited, while post-crisis audits would ensure that all relaxed standards are temporary, restoring full democratic accountability once the emergency passes.

Strategic industrial investments must extend beyond ammunition. Semiconductors, rare earths, and specialty chemicals underpin modern military operations and cannot be treated as ordinary market commodities. Redundant domestic facilities are essential to prevent single points of failure. Complementing this, allied nations must be integrated into formal supply chain agreements, allowing shared inventories and coordinated surge production. These investments should be sustained, predictable, and multi-year, rather than reactive, one-off projects. To ensure these funds are not diverted, a dedicated Industrial Resilience Fund (IRF) could be established, ring-fenced, perhaps 5-10% of the total defense procurement budget, exclusively focused on industrial redundancy, modernization, and surge capacity incentives. Framed this way, the fund is not a discretionary expense but a strategic insurance premium for national and alliance security.

Human capital is a critical, often underappreciated element of industrial resilience. Temporary adjustments to labor and licensing regulations are necessary, but a more enduring solution is a "Strategic Industrial Reserve." By establishing formal links between the defense industrial base and vocational schools or community colleges, governments can pre-certify a reserve pool of skilled welders, chemical technicians, and machinists who could be rapidly mobilized in a crisis. This approach addresses the long lead times associated with specialized labor, ensuring that surge capacity is not constrained by workforce shortages.

NATO and other alliance structures offer additional opportunities for reform. Industrial capacity should be treated as a collective defense asset, comparable to standing forces. Agreements on resource allocation, rapid contracting, and logistics coordination can ensure that no single nation bears the burden of surge production alone. Standardized reporting of production capacity and inventories, along with joint industrial exercises simulating crisis mobilization, would stress-test readiness and inform permanent improvements.

A recurring challenge throughout the ammunition enterprise is the lack of systematic institutional memory. Lessons learned at one facility often fail to inform decisions elsewhere, resulting in repeated mistakes.

Centralized repositories for best practices, structured knowledge sharing across facilities, and mandatory post-project reviews would ensure that operational experience accumulates rather than dissipates with personnel turnover. Such mechanisms would also strengthen coordination across allied supply chains, enabling faster and more efficient mobilization.

Financial and strategic considerations are inseparable from these reforms. Multi-year, ring-fenced budget commitments, such as the IRF, are essential not only to maintain peacetime readiness but to guarantee rapid surge capacity when needed. Investments in redundancy, zoning, modernization, and human capital should be framed as insurance against operational failure: the cost of being unprepared far exceeds the upfront outlay required to maintain industrial resilience. Industrial readiness metrics must also directly inform force planning, operational concepts, and strategic commitments, aligning military ambitions with the realities of production capability.

The challenge facing Western democracies is clear: maintaining accountability and transparency while achieving industrial agility. Without deliberate reforms, bureaucratic bottlenecks, coordination failures, and outdated procedures will continue to limit responsiveness, leaving forces vulnerable even when financial and technological resources are abundant. By establishing flexible regulatory frameworks, investing in resilient industrial infrastructure, integrating allied capacities, institutionalizing lessons learned, and building a ready industrial workforce, the West can begin to close the gap between potential and practice.

The stakes are profound. Adversaries unconstrained by democratic oversight are increasingly capable of rapid industrial mobilization. To maintain strategic parity, Western military establishments must accept that capability follows strategy. Reforms are neither simple nor quick, but they are essential to ensuring that democratic forces can respond decisively in the twenty-first century's prolonged and complex conflicts.

CONCLUSION

The Invariant Equation Of Strategic Sustainability

The preceding analysis, spanning production bottlenecks, supply chain vulnerabilities, organizational dysfunction, and mobilization constraints, converges on a deceptively simple relationship that governs strategic sustainability in modern warfare. This relationship can be expressed as an invariant: **Strategic Capacity = Production Rate × Operational Time × Replenishment Efficiency.**[1] Every factor in this equation imposes absolute limits that no amount of tactical brilliance, technological sophistication, or operational innovation can overcome.

Production rate represents the maximum sustainable output of munitions, replacement equipment, and consumables that industrial systems can generate under optimal conditions. As documented throughout this book, Western production rates for critical items like artillery munitions remain substantially below the consumption rates observed during high-intensity operations in Ukraine. The European Union output of about two million artillery rounds annually by early 2025, while representing genuine industrial mobilization, covers roughly two-thirds to nine-tenths of the peak daily consumption seen in 2022. United States production increases from 14,000 to over 40,000 155mm shells monthly represent impressive scaling but remain constrained by workforce limitations, supply chain dependencies, and regulatory processes that cannot be infinitely compressed.

Operational time introduces the temporal dimension that transforms production constraints into strategic vulnerabilities. Stockpiles accumulated over years can be exhausted in weeks during intensive combat. Replacement cycles for precision-guided munitions extend across 18-36 months while these systems are consumed in hours or days of deployment. The temporal asymmetry between consumption and replenishment creates operational feedback loops where commanders must ration resources based on anticipated replenishment timelines rather than immediate tactical requirements. More critically, adversaries who maintain excess production capacity or who can activate surge manufacturing more rapidly than Western democracies gain advantages that compound over time, advantages that become decisive in conflicts extending beyond initial stockpile exhaustion.

Replenishment efficiency captures the multiplicity of factors that determine whether theoretical production capacity translates into actual operational availability. Regulatory approvals, environmental reviews, safety certifications, security clearances, and procurement procedures all introduce friction that extends timelines and constrains throughput. Supply chain disruptions, whether from natural disasters, cyberattacks, or deliberate adversary interdiction, can sever critical inputs and halt production regardless of facility capacity. Organizational dysfunction, from unclear lines of authority to inadequate lessons-learned processes, generates coordination failures that waste resources and delay capability improvements. Human capital constraints impose ceilings on how rapidly production can scale even when facilities and funding are available.

The strategic implication of this invariant equation is that military capabilities must be assessed not merely through platform counts or technological sophistication but through rigorous analysis of sustainable production rates, realistic operational timelines, and honest evaluation of replenishment efficiency given actual regulatory, supply chain, and organizational constraints. Forces that appear formidable when assessed through traditional metrics may prove incapable of sustained operations when industrial capacity cannot replace consumed munitions at rates matching operational tempo.

The Ukraine conflict has provided an empirical demonstration of how this equation constrains strategic possibility. Ukrainian forces equipped with Western artillery systems and trained by NATO instructors have proven tactically effective, yet their operational capabilities have been limited not by crew proficiency or platform performance but by munitions availability determined by Western production capacity. Ukraine's fire ratio, roughly 1 to 3 by mid-2025, reflects not Ukrainian tactical choices but industrial mathematics: the combined output of Western munitions production cannot match the sustained consumption rates that high-intensity conflict demands.

The dependencies documented in Chapter 10 add a critical dimension to this equation: replenishment efficiency approaches zero if supply chains are severed. The discovery of Chinese components in F-35 aircraft, the concentration of microelectronics manufacturing in Taiwan, and the pervasive foreign sources in munitions supply chains collectively reveal that Western production capacity depends on continued access to suppliers that potential adversaries may control or influence. A conflict scenario that disrupts these supply chains would simultaneously create peak demand for precision munitions while eliminating access to components essential for their manufacture, a paradox that no amount of stockpiling can resolve if conflicts extend beyond stockpile exhaustion timelines.

The equation is not abstract, it dictates the tempo and endurance of entire alliances. When the rate, time, or efficiency term collapses, so does operational credibility.

The policy implications flowing from this invariant equation are clear but politically challenging. First, peacetime production rates and strategic stockpiles must be sized to sustain operations without assuming that mobilization can provide surge capacity comparable to World War II precedents. The regulatory, workforce, and supply chain constraints documented throughout this book mean that rapid scaling remains infeasible within operationally relevant timescales. Second, supply chain dependencies on potential adversaries must be systematically identified and mitigated even when near-term costs appear prohibitive. The temporal dimension matters critically: investments initiated today to reduce dependencies will not mature for years, yet conflicts can begin with minimal warning. Third, organizational reforms addressing the bureaucratic dysfunctions documented in Chapter 9 are not administrative minutiae but strategic imperatives, unclear lines of authority and inadequate coordination mechanisms constrain industrial capacity as effectively as insufficient funding.

Fourth, alliance burden-sharing must explicitly incorporate industrial capacity as a collective defense asset rather than treating production as each nation's domestic concern. NATO's response to Ukrainian munitions requirements has demonstrated both the potential and limitations of alliance industrial cooperation. Systematic integration of production planning, supply chain coordination, and surge capacity development across allied nations could partially compensate for individual nations' constraints, but this requires mechanisms and agreements extending far beyond current alliance structures.

Fifth, operational concepts and force employment strategies must be designed around realistic assessments of sustainable consumption rates rather than optimistic assumptions about replenishment. Commanders who must ration precision munitions because production cannot match consumption face fundamentally different tactical choices than those operating with assured replenishment. Acknowledging these constraints in doctrine, training, and operational planning is not defeatism but realism, the alternative is discovering limitations only when conflicts have begun and adaptation opportunities have narrowed.

The uncomfortable conclusion emerging from this analysis is that Western military establishments have constructed force structures and undertaken alliance commitments that their industrial bases cannot sustain during prolonged high-intensity conflicts. The technological sophistication of weapons systems, the training proficiency of personnel, and the tactical doctrine guiding operations are necessary but insufficient for strategic success when industrial capacity cannot generate the munitions these forces require. Adversaries aware of these constraints can structure their own industrial policies, operational concepts, and strategic choices to exploit temporal asymmetries and production vulnerabilities that Western planning has systematically underestimated.

Addressing these vulnerabilities requires confronting difficult trade-offs between efficiency and resilience, cost-effectiveness and redundancy, peacetime optimization and wartime surge capacity. Democratic societies that have spent three decades prioritizing lean operations, regulatory compliance, and market-based allocation of defense production must now consider whether these approaches remain adequate in an international environment where adversaries deliberately maintain excess industrial capacity as strategic insurance. The investments required, in facilities, workforce development, supply chain diversification, and regulatory reform, are substantial and will compete with other defense priorities in constrained budgets.

Yet the costs of failing to address industrial capacity constraints are potentially catastrophic. Alliance commitments become hollow when the industrial capacity to sustain them is absent. Deterrence loses credibility when adversaries recognize that Western forces cannot be sustained beyond initial stockpile exhaustion. Operational plans become fantasy when they assume munitions availability that production capacity cannot provide. The mathematical relationship between production rate, operational time, and replenishment efficiency is not a theoretical construct but an empirical reality that will determine strategic outcomes regardless of whether defense establishments acknowledge it in their planning.

The invariant equation of strategic sustainability, Strategic Capacity = Production Rate × Operational Time × Replenishment Efficiency, represents the fundamental constraint that shapes what is militarily possible in the twenty-first century. Understanding this equation and its implications is not optional for defense establishments that seek to maintain strategic relevance in an era where industrial capacity has become a decisive determinant of military effectiveness. The Ukraine conflict has provided the empirical evidence that should compel this recognition. Whether Western democracies respond with the industrial investments, organizational reforms, and strategic reorientations that these realities demand will determine whether their military advantages prove sustainable or ephemeral when confronted with adversaries who have already internalized these lessons and structured their entire defense economies around them.

References

All quantitative data in this book derive from publicly available government, industry, and research-institute publications between 2022 and 2025. No classified or restricted materials were used.

- Government Accountability Office (2023). Army Ammunition: Organizational and Oversight Challenges Persist. GAO-23-106 457.
- European Commission (2025, April 9). One Million Shells Delivered Under ASAP Plan. IP/25/178.
- U.S. Department of Defense (2024, Oct 20). 155 mm Ammunition Production Briefing. Pentagon Press Office.
- Bureau of Labor Statistics (2024). Employment Projections 2030.
- TrendForce (2025). Global Foundry Capacity Report Q1 2025.
- U.S. Geological Survey (2025). Mineral Commodities Summary: Rare Earths.
- UK Ministry of Defence (2024 Dec). Defense Intelligence Update: Ammunition Production.
- Republic of Korea Ministry of National Defense (2025 Feb). Defense White Paper 2025.

www.ingramcontent.com/pod-product-compliance
Lightning Source LLC
LaVergne TN
LVHW090422210926
848480LV00002B/650
* 9 7 9 8 2 3 3 3 7 3 1 2 1 *